THE MASTER GARDENER'S GUIDE TO

PATIOS
& CONTAINERS

How to create and care for your own
patio garden

ALAN TOOGOOD

SELECT
EDITIONS

A SALAMANDER BOOK

This edition published 1991 by Selectabook Ltd.,
Folly Road,
Roundway,
Devizes,
Wiltshire, U.K.
SN10 2HR.

ISBN 0 86101 240 2

All correspondence concerning the content of this volume should be addressed to Salamander Books Ltd.

Credits

Editor: John Woodward
Designer: Kathy Gummer
Copy editor: Jonathan Hilton
Filmset: Modern Text Ltd.

Colour reproductions:
Rodney Howe Ltd.
Printed in Belgium by
Henri Proost & Cie, Turnhout

AUTHOR

Alan Toogood trained at the Royal Botanic Gardens at Kew, Surrey and the Parks and Gardens Department at Brighton, Sussex, before going on to a two-year studentship at the Royal Horticultural Society's garden at Wisley, Surrey. He worked as a horticultural journalist on *Gardeners' Chronicle* and *Amateur Gardening* magazines, and later became Lecturer in Horticulture and Nursery Practices at Merrist Wood Agricultural College. For several years he was Editor of the monthly magazine *Greenhouse*. He is now a freelance horticultural journalist and consultant, the author of many gardening books, and Horticulture Correspondent for *The Times*.

Consultant
Ann Bonar has been a horticultural writer and consultant for more than 20 years, and has written many books on various aspects of gardening. She is a regular contributor to a variety of gardening periodicals and trade journals, and has taken part in a number of gardening programmes broadcast by the BBC. For 12 years she has answered readers' queries sent in to a leading British weekly gardening magazine.

CONTENTS

INTRODUCTION

Growing plants in containers has been practised since Roman times, and has probably never been more popular than it is today, yet there seems little information available on suitable plants and their cultivation. This book is intended to fill that gap.

Plants in containers can bring a splash of welcome colour to patios, terraces, roof gardens and balconies; while hanging baskets or other elevated containers can enhance walls and brighten up window sills.

Patios represent a very important extension of our living space, and today most gardens have one, even if it is only tiny. In this book you will find many ideas for patio designs as well as other features, such as double walls for plants, raised beds and pools. Also considered is the wide range of flooring materials currently available.

The choice of plant containers is truly vast, ranging from simple pots to elaborate urns; from window boxes, troughs and grow-bags, to sinks and hanging containers. Matching container

Above: *Window boxes provide a means of brightening up window-sills and can be planted with spring or summer bedding. Here daffodils and tender cinerarias welcome the spring.*
Right: *Summer bedding plants in tubs and urns bring welcome colour to many parts of the garden, including patios and terraces.*
Far right: *The surrounds of a patio should be bright and cheerful. Again one can use seasonal bedding, like this summer scheme of alyssum, lobelia, marigolds and pelargoniums. Mass planting ensures really strong impact.*

and planting scheme is vital, not only to the overall appearance of your patio but also to the health of the plants.

As well as a wealth of design ideas, all the relevant practical aspects, such as suitable composts and soils, tools and equipment, filling and planting containers are covered, as well as all aspects of plant care, from watering to pruning and propagation.

The many plants suitable for containers, and for planting in and around the patio, are recommended and described. These include herbaceous perennials and bedding plants, shrubs, fruits and vegetables.

Many of the ideas here will, hopefully, appeal to disabled people. Raised beds and double walls for plants, for example, can be easily maintained from wheelchairs. Indeed, a flat, well-paved patio garden is ideal for those confined to wheelchairs.

People who live in flats and apartments will certainly appreciate the ideas for balcony and roof gardening.

Virtually every garden has a special area for sitting out, and this is generally referred to as a patio. It is an ideal spot for growing plants, too, especially in containers. Another aspect of your home, the front entrance, is probably in full view of passers by—so make sure it looks attractive, and again use plants in pots and tubs as a decorative feature.

THE PATIO

The correct meaning of patio is an inner courtyard (see pp.18-19), but today we use the term to describe any paved or hard area in the garden, which is used for sitting, relaxing and entertaining.
Siting: Invariably, a patio is positioned next to the house, or nearby. In any event it should be in a sunny sheltered spot.

If further shelter or even privacy is required, the patio could be partially enclosed with a screen. A pierced screen-block wall, for instance, or trellis or fencing panels, make ideal supports for growing climbing plants.
Shape: Many people are not adventurous enough when it comes to the shape of their patio—sticking to a square or rectangle. But there is no reason why a patio should not be any

Above: *A patio can be any shape desired. This circular one in brick would surely look good in many gardens, and is easy to lay.*

shape—very irregular if desired. There are many materials to use for its construction (see pp.38-39). A brick edging to the patio looks good, especially if it butts up to the lawn.
Planting areas: Provide plenty of planting areas both in and around the patio, otherwise it may look rather bare. For a more informal look, include planting areas in the corners. Large-leaved and 'architectural' plants look attractive, giving a lush, tropical appearance. Examples are the phormiums and the hardy types of yucca.

When laying the patio floor, leave some gaps for planting creeping and mat-forming plants, such as thymes, aubrieta and raoulias.
Special features: Double walls surrounding or partially surrounding a patio create an attractive feature (see pp.32-33).

A sunken formal pool with a bubble fountain provides the relaxing sound of moving water and the chance to grow some more unusual plants.

Another idea is a timber pergola. This could be built to

Above: *Of unusual shape, but not difficult to construct, this brick patio has been designed with planting areas around it.*

Above: *A colourful front entrance provides a welcome for visitors. Skilful use has been made of hanging baskets, summer bedding plants and a conifer in a tub: all easy to achieve.*

partially cover the patio—with a climber such as a grape vine trained over it, to provide shade from the heat of the day.

ENTRANCES

It is a good idea to keep the front entrance to the house fairly simple and uncluttered. Quite impressive are tubs of clipped bay, or conifers, each side of the front door.

Plantings along the front path and near the door should ideally be kept low, using lots of mat and hummock-forming plants, dwarf lavender being one of the favourites. Choose plants, too, that do not mind being trodden on. **The porch:** The porch and windows can be highly decorative if you use hanging baskets, wall baskets and window boxes filled with summer bedding plants.

If you have an enclosed porch consider displaying tender houseplants for the summer, or fuchsias and pelargoniums. In winter and spring use hardy plants, such as bowls of spring bulbs, alpines in pans, and small potted foliage shrubs, such as variegated aucuba and *Fatsia japonica.* Porches are becoming very fashionable today and many people like to use them like mini-conservatories!

11

WINDOWSILLS AND BALCONIES

Generally, passers-by enjoy displays in window boxes and on balconies just as much as the owners and, therefore, you should be conscious of creating really eye-catching displays. Use bright and strong colours, in solid masses, wherever possible.

COLOURFUL WINDOWSILLS

Generally plants are grown in window boxes on the windowsill, but for further colour around the windows there is no reason why hanging baskets and wall baskets should not be used. Tubs of plants can also be placed on the ground below the windows.

WINDOW BOXES

Whichever planting schemes you choose, do avoid plants all of the same height down the whole length of the box. This will result in a very uniform and uninteresting display.

Instead, aim for height at one end, graduating to lower plants and trailing kinds at the other end. Alternatively, use tall plants in the centre, graduating to lower plants and trailers at each end of the box.

There are plenty of colourful bedding plants for summer colour, and bedding plants and

Above: *A very wide range of plants can be used in window boxes. This one contains begonias and petunias.*

bulbs for the spring. These are, of course, temporary, and in some boxes you may prefer permanent plantings. Here are some ideas for both, listed in the order, tall to low.

PERMANENT SCHEMES

● Dwarf conifers with bluish or greyish foliage and golden-leaved heathers (varieties of *Calluna vulgaris*).
● Dwarf golden-leaved conifers and variegated trailing ivies and periwinkles.
● Dwarf conifers, such as *Juniperus communis* 'Compressa', alpines, and miniature bulbs.

TEMPORARY SCHEMES

● Summer—bush fuchsias, *Begonia semperflorens*, trailing fuchsias.
● Summer—zonal pelargoniums, ageratum and begonias, ivy-leaved pelargoniums.
● Summer—variegated abutilons, zonal pelargoniums mixed with silver-leaved cineraria, chlorophytum.
● Summer—climbing *Thunbergia alata*, and trailing nasturtiums.

Above: *This small conservatory undoubtedly extends the scope of balcony gardening.*

- Summer—climbing ipomoea, French marigolds, trailing petunias.
- Spring—small plants of variegated aucuba, double early tulips, trailing aubrieta.
- Spring—tulips, polyanthus and trailing aubrieta.
- Winter—winter-flowering pansies, with hyacinths for spring.

COLOURFUL BALCONIES

Plants can be grown in large planters of lightweight fibreglass, tubs made of fibreglass or plastic, and in growing-bags. Use light-weight, soilless compost.

Most plants should be arranged at the outer edge where there will be more light. There may well be poor light towards the back of the balcony so plants which do not mind shade should be grown here. A bay tree, for example, in a tub would give fair results, as would fuchsias grown as standards or other trained forms, begonias and polyanthus. Some of the tougher houseplants, which need shade from direct sun, could be arranged on staging of some kind for the summer.

Window boxes could, if safely secured, be positioned on top of the balcony walls and planted out with summer and spring bedding, using plenty of trailing plants to cascade over the sides and front of the balcony.

TRELLIS SCREENS

To give privacy, a degree of wind protection and support for climbing plants, it may be possible to erect a trellis screen at, say, one end of the balcony. The trellis can be painted or left in its natural state.

BASKETS

Hanging baskets, fixed from the roof at the front of the balcony, are another colourful idea. Make good use of any solid walls by installing wall baskets.

MINI-GREENHOUSE

There are currently several mini-greenhouses available, ideally suited to balconies, which can be used for plant raising and, perhaps, for overwintering tender plants. These can also be used for displaying houseplants in the summer months, and should be positioned in a sunny spot if this is possible.

It is possible to create delightful gardens on flat roofs despite such problems as wind and rapid drying of soil. Simple schemes are probably the most pleasing, using tough plants and lightweight construction materials.

THE FIRST STEP

First of all the roof must be checked for loading (to assess how much weight it can take), to ensure waterproofing properties are not affected, and to ensure surplus water is able to drain away correctly.

This means liaising with the local authority planning department, and perhaps enlisting the professional advice of an architect or structural engineer before any work is undertaken.

A SIMPLE DESIGN

It seems more appropriate to keep the layout of the garden fairly simple. In this respect you could copy the Japanese—perhaps not a true Japanese garden, but at least a design that creates the 'flavour' of one, including restrained use of colour.

The main plantings could be in raised beds, perhaps built up with lightweight blocks, timber, peat blocks, or even large fibreglass planters.

The beds, filled with lightweight compost, could contain plants that give the flavour of Japan, including Japanese maples (varieties of *Acer palmatum*); the sacred bamboo or *Nandina domestica* with large compound leaves (provide it with a sheltered spot); real bamboos; prostrate junipers, particularly to 'soften' the edges of the beds; ornamental grasses; dwarf pines; and the dwarf evergreen Kurume azaleas, which flower in spring and need acid soil.

CREATING AN ATTRACTIVE FLOOR

The floor of your roof garden could be covered with a layer of lightweight aggregate—perhaps

using several colours in different parts of the garden. If you do not like walking on the aggregate, put down some lightweight slabs to act as stepping stones. Another idea for a flooring surface is synthetic plastic turf—some look remarkably natural.

FOCAL POINTS

Weight permitting, a group of attractively shaped rocks could be made into a typically Japanese feature. An ideal material for this is tufa—a natural, lightweight volcanic rock.

Stone lanterns, overhung with Japanese maple, and basins could be used to create further focal points. A basin filled with water could be surrounded with damp-loving ferns.

A WATER FEATURE

A slightly raised, shallow pool of irregular shape could be easily formed with a butyl-rubber pool liner. Black is the best colour. The sound of moving water would

Above: *Coloured shingle and slabs form a distinctive 'floor'.*
Left: *A simple, yet effective roof garden in the Japanese style, featuring a raised bed.*

make this feature even more enjoyable, and this could be provided by means of a bubble fountain (not a tall one since this looks rather unnatural).

Alternatively water could be made to trickle into the pool over smooth pebbles. Moving water is easily achieved with an electric submersible pump.

GENERAL CONSIDERATIONS

As in a normal garden it is a good idea if possible to divide the garden, or screen off parts, so that the whole cannot be seen in one glance. This could be achieved in the roof garden by erecting some screens formed of bamboo. Climbing plants could then be trained over them.

All materials used in a roof garden must, of course, be light in weight, including any paving slabs or building blocks. Use lightweight compost for the beds and containers, such as an all-peat potting compost. These composts do not, however, retain moisture very well, and so dry out more rapidly than soil-based types.

The problem can be partly solved by ensuring a good depth of compost: 6in (15cm) should be considered as a minimum for herbaceous plants, alpines, bulbs, annuals and small shrubs, and 12in (30cm) for large shrubs and small trees. Pay frequent attention to watering, though, especially during hot spells, and feed all plants regularly.

Roof gardens can sometimes be windy, especially if they are high up. To help provide protection, transparent barriers could be erected around the boundary, perhaps on top of the walls. Use, for instance, clear or tinted plastic panels or even 'frosted' panels if you want privacy or to hide an ugly view. Alternatively, timber trellis panels filter the wind and provide a framework on which to grow climbers, and these make a very attractive windbreak.

BASEMENTS AND BACKYARDS

A garden can be created in any area, however small or heavily shaded. Even a basement yard in the middle of town can be transformed into a delightful garden retreat by imaginative use of the space available.

BASEMENT GARDENS

Most people aim to pack as many plants as possible into the small area. One way of achieving this is to erect tiered timber staging against one or more basement walls—the slatted type often used in greenhouses for displaying pot plants is ideal. Any excess water will simply drain harmlessly away through the slats, so minimizing the possibility of rot. If you don't want to buy proprietary greenhouse staging, you can make your own from western red cedar.

USING THE WALLS

In most basements there is plenty of wall space, which can be used for hanging baskets and various other wall containers.

The walls can also be clothed with climbing plants such as honeysuckles and clematis, which will not mind if the area is on the shady side. These could be planted in deep wooden or concrete containers. Around the base of the climbers plant some smaller subjects—perhaps miniature bulbs or trailing alpines.

Above: *A well-planned backyard.*
Left: *A basement with grape vine, Passion flower and fuchsias.*

COPING WITH SHADE

If the basement is in complete shade, plants will have to be chosen with care. Suitable subjects include *Begonia semperflorens*, mimulus, impatiens, and possibly fuchsias and marigolds if the shade is not too dense. For spring try daffodils, polyanthus and forget-me-nots. There are many shrubs for shade, including dwarf junipers and yews, winter jasmine and skimmias.

Painting the basement walls in a light colour will make best use of any light that is available.

SMALL BACKYARDS

A tiny pocket-handkerchief plot can be made into a delightful garden. Usually it is best to pave most of the area. If you have children and make heavy use of the garden, grass is not a practical proposition: it will soon become 'threadbare', or turn into a mud patch in winter.

However, a contrast in texture can be achieved with gravel

areas formed of pea shingle, available from builder's merchants. Use it around the bases of ornamental pots, containing temporary or permanent plants.

A large trough or raised bed will provide a welcome variation in height and can be used for all kinds of plants, including spring and summer bedding.

A SITTING AREA

To make an attractive sitting area, a timber pergola could be built against a wall of the house. The floor may be paved or it could be timber decking to give a warm cosy feeling and to contrast with paving in the rest of the garden. Climbers can be grown up and over the pergola, perhaps to create shade if it is a hot sunny spot. A good choice is a hardy grape vine such as *Vitis vinifera* 'Brant'. Any paved area butting up to the house must be kept below the level of the damp-proof course.

RAISED FEATURES

Another idea for a backyard is to use several raised features to create interest. A raised pool is easily constructed to the required height with ornamental walling blocks, and the inside lined with butyl-rubber pool liner. The walls of the pool could be made wide enough to sit on and finished off with coping stones, cemented firmly in place.

A raised bed, made from either wood, bricks or, for a more informal appearance, irregular-shaped stones for plants. This would look good planted with bold, dramatic subjects such as a hardy palm, ornamental grasses, yuccas and phormiums, with prostrate junipers cascading over the edges. This theme could be repeated in ornamental tubs, pots and urns. Phormiums and yuccas, especially, are excellent plants for containers in less-cold areas.

COURTYARDS

A courtyard is an area open to the sky but surrounded by walls or buildings. It may be enclosed on all sides or only on two or three. The true courtyard, as found in ancient Greek and Roman times, was completely surrounded by the house, with all the rooms leading on to it. Rather special treatment is recommended if you are lucky enough to own a courtyard.

CONSIDERING A THEME

In warm climates the courtyard is a cool, sheltered, private retreat where you can gain relief from the heat of the day.

The ancient Greeks and Romans grew trees in their court-yards, plants in large terracotta containers, and further enhanced the area with statues. Simplicity, though, was the keynote, and it is not a bad idea to stick to this concept in the modern courtyard. A few plants in containers, a pool with a fountain, and a table and chairs may be sufficient to create a quiet, restful retreat from the bustling modern world.

THE FLOOR

In Mediterranean courtyards the floor is often paved with marble slabs. Marble could be used for a new courtyard, although it is expensive. A cheaper alternative is square concrete paving slabs. These can be monotonous used over a large area if all one colour, so consider black and white (or dark grey and light grey) slabs, laid in a chequer-board pattern.

POOL AND FOUNTAIN

It would be hard to suggest something better than a pool and fountain as a central feature. This creates a cool atmosphere and the sound of moving water is, to most people, very relaxing.

In a courtyard, a raised pool is suggested, certainly formal,

and either round or square. The walls of the pool should be capped with coping stones and these could be used as an additional seating area, and a good vantage point from which to admire the waterlilies and fish in the pool.

A stone fountain could be positioned in the centre of the pool—the more elaborate the better. Three-tier stone fountains are available, with bowls, so the water cascades from one to the other into the pool. This gives a more pleasing effect than jets of water springing up from the surface.

GREENERY

There should be plants, but not of such quantity as to create jungle-like conditions. The majority could be large-leaved foliage plants to give a lush sub-tropical atmosphere. By all means have some flowering plants, too, to provide splashes of colour here and there.

Plants will be grown in containers—you can go to town

Below: *Statuary and an oleander grown in a tub help to create a Mediterranean effect in this attractive courtyard.*

Above: *Every courtyard should have a pool and fountain as a central feature to create a 'cool' atmosphere in which to relax.*

here with all kinds of urns and vases in classical designs— none would be too elaborate in such a setting. Ideally, to create impact, place containers in groups instead of dotting them about singly.

Foliage plants to be recommended include the hardy palm (*Trachycarpus fortunei*); plantain lilies or hostas; and the evergreen shrub *Fatsia japonica.* All of these will tolerate some shade.

For sunny spots try citrus fruits in tubs, overwintering them under glass or indoors. Other fruits that could be grown outdoors in pots all year round are trained figs and grape vines. These, too, need sun.

The white arum lily (*Zantedeschia aethiopica*) makes a good container plant and has bold foliage and white flowers. The tender cannas have bold foliage, too, and brilliant lily-like heads of flowers. They need full sun. For cool shady spots there are many hardy ferns, such as *Asplenium trichomanes,* to choose from.

CLOTHING THE WALLS

Good use should be made of all available wall space, perhaps providing white trellis panels to support the plants. For a warm sunny wall, grow a grape vine, a trained fig or a passion flower (*Passiflora caerulea*). Shady walls could be clothed with large-leaved variegated ivies, fragrant jasmine or the white-flowered climbing hydrangea (*H. petiolaris*).

FLOWER POTS

The ubiquitous 'flower pot' can be used both for raising young plants and for display work on patios and terraces. It is surprising, though, how many versions are now available.

CLAY POTS

The traditional terracotta clay pot is a pleasing, orange-brown colour, available in a wide range of sizes from about 2in (5cm) in diameter to 12-14in (30-35·5cm). There are also giant ones with diameters of 18-24in (45-61cm). As well as traditional plain English pots, there are fancy or decorated ones in the style of Venetian or Florentine, Tuscan and Minoan earthenware. These are usually large, for display work. There are also glazed terracotta pots available which, although attractive, are not porous and can inhibit growth.

Clay pans, about one-third of the height of pots, are often used for growing alpines and for seed growing, and half-pots (about half the height of normal ones) are ideal for low-growing plants.

It is safe to say that all plants look 'at home' in clays and you can use them for propagating and growing-on plants. For display work, do not use any smaller than 6in (15cm) in diameter; smaller ones dry out extremely quickly.

Above: *Terracotta clay pots are available in plain or fancy designs and in many sizes.*

Pots 6in (15cm) and upwards in diameter are recommended for all permanent plants—shrubs, fruits, large perennials, and so on.
Pros and cons: Clays are porous so surplus moisture is quickly lost, and compost does not stay wet; they can dry out quickly in hot weather; they are suitable for plants needing a well-drained soil; due to their weight clays are ideal for large or heavy plants. On the other hand they are easily broken; they can be damaged by frost; they are also not too easy to clean.

PLASTIC POTS

These are available in a similar range of sizes to clays, including half-pots and pans. Most plants look best in the traditional terracotta colour plastic pot, but the black pots can also be attractive.
Pros and cons: Plastic pots are a good choice for plants that like moist conditions, as the compost does not dry out rapidly; they are not an ideal choice, though, for those plants needing good drainage, such as alpines and bulbs. After a number of years plastics can become brittle, so they are easily cracked or broken;

the compost can remain wet for a long time if you are heavy-handed with watering; a combination of plastic pot and soilless compost results in a very light unit, so large plants may be blown over; they are, however, relatively inexpensive to buy.

OTHER TYPES OF POT

Compressed peat: These are designed for plant raising, and the pot is planted with the plant so there is no root disturbance. They are ideal for raising bedding plants and vegetables, since you can plant seedlings direct into the pots. The compost, though, is

Below: *All plants look 'at home' in clay pots, including the colourful summer bedding plants.*

liable to dry out quickly. The most useful size is 3-3½in (7·5-9cm) in diameter. Do not attempt to remove plants from peat pots, since the roots grow into the pot walls.

Plastic bags: Flexible black polythene bags are much used for growing-on young plants. They are cheaper than normal pots, but can be used once only, being slit and peeled off before the contents are planted. Use them for growing summer bedding plants and vegetables.

Whalehides: These are bituminized paper pots available in the same sizes as peat pots, and they have the same uses. Again, the pot is planted with the plant. Larger versions are available for growing plants like tomatoes, but they will only last for one season.

WINDOW BOXES, TROUGHS AND URNS

Window boxes give character to any house, and troughs add variety to the patio or terrace. There are probably few containers better than urns and jars for creating focal points and for providing a 'Mediterranean' atmosphere.

WINDOW BOXES

These can be bought from a garden centre and may be made of traditional wood, plastic and, expensive but most attractive, terracotta clay. If you are an accomplished carpenter you will no doubt find it easy to make your own, to fit the width of your house or apartment windows. Wooden ones can, of course, be painted to match the colour scheme of the windows.

To ensure the boxes retain moisture, the minimum depth and width should be 10in (25cm). The length will depend on the window, but if your windows are 6ft (1·8m) wide, it may be better to have two 3ft (90cm) boxes.

If you do not wish to paint wooden boxes, then at least treat them inside and out with a clear horticultural wood preservative.

To ensure good drainage, the boxes should ideally be raised slightly above the windowsills. However, if they are to stand on the windowsills, and the sills slope, then provide wedges underneath the front edges of the boxes. It goes without saying that window boxes must be supported with strong brackets firmly fixed to the house—black wrought iron looks particularly effective.

Top: *Wrought-iron brackets make good window-box supports.*
Above: *Strong 'ties' will support boxes on narrow sills.*

Top: *Sloping window-sills need not be a problem for boxes.*
Above: *Brackets supporting a box on a balcony wall.*

Bear in mind that window boxes can be used, too, on the tops of walls, including balcony walls—in this instance they may need drip trays underneath them. This would also apply to boxes on the windowsills of flats.

Suitable plants for boxes include bulbs of all kinds, especially spring-flowering types, hardy and half-hardy annuals, spring bedding plants, or permanent displays of low-growing perennials, alpines or shrubs.

TROUGHS

These are usually long, rectangular plant containers of a good depth. There are many designs to choose from; they may be made from timber, concrete or fibreglass and some are made to imitate classical designs. Old stone troughs are much sought after, but it is possible to buy new ones.

Unless they are provided with legs, troughs are best raised on bricks or blocks of wood to ensure good drainage.

Choice of plants for troughs is the same as for window boxes.

Below: *Urns come in a variety of shapes and materials, including terracotta and lead. Some clay urns have a glazed finish.*

LOW, FLAT BOWLS

Low, flat, concrete bowls became popular in the early 1950s, and are still popular today. They look good in very modern surroundings and ideally should be planted with brightly coloured flowers, such as summer bedding (especially trailing pelargoniums and petunias). For early colour, plant with spring bedding, or bulbs such as tulips.

URNS AND JARS

Urns and jars often have fairly narrow necks, which can be a disadvantage, since few plants look in proportion to the container. However, they are marvellous for using as focal points and for creating a sun-drenched atmosphere on the patio or terrace.

Urns are often shaped like the funerary urns of the ancient Romans and Greeks, and have been popular for garden decoration since the seventeenth century.

For a different effect, try raising urns above eye-level—on piers, for example, or on a wall.

Urns and jars look good when planted with trailing petunias or ivy-leaved pelargoniums and, if there is space, with a taller plant in the centre, such as a young *Cordyline australis.*

TUBS, PLANTERS AND BARRELS

For large deep containers look to the range of tubs, planters and barrels available at most garden centres. Often they are very decorative and suitable for permanent plants or seasonal bedding displays. Designs are available for formal modern settings as well as for the patios or terraces of period houses and country gardens.

TUBS

Basically tubs are large, deep containers that can be used for sizeable permanent plants, such as shrubs, trees and climbers. They are also popular for displays of spring and summer bedding plants.

Tubs are available in various materials, but wood is a good choice for a hot place—the soil moisture takes longer to evaporate and so the compost dries out less quickly.

Tubs can be bought as cut-down barrels from garden centres. These need to be treated with a horticultural timber preservative before use, and holes drilled in the base for drainage.

Purpose-made ornamental timber tubs are also available and may be round or square. Square tubs are recommended for trees and large shrubs. The traditional square wooden tub had removable side panels to allow for easy removal of the plant when it needed a fresh supply of compost. Traditional-style wooden tubs are still available but the sides are not usually removable. If you want this facility it will be a case of making your own.

Many people like to paint wooden tubs, but there are few colours which look 'right' in the garden. White or grey, however, would be a good choice.

Concrete tubs are easy to come by and they are a suitable choice for a modern setting. But for informal settings consider real or imitation stone.

Tubs come in various sizes, and

Above: *White petunias and ivies in a wooden tub. Wood is a good choice for hot places as the compost does not dry out quickly, so plants grow much better.*

the most useful of these are 20in (50cm) across by 18in (45·5cm) high, and 16in (40cm) across by 14in (35·5cm) high.

It is best to stand tubs on blocks of wood or bricks to raise them off the ground slightly, since this ensures better drainage of any surplus water.

PLANTERS

These are very large containers intended for groups of plants —shrubs, for example, and perennials together. But they can also be used for bedding, bulbs and the like. They give you greater scope for a variety of planting schemes than, say, tubs.

The true planter is a portable

container, either square or rectangular, and made in timber, fibreglass or plastic. Of course, you may prefer to make your own timber planter, using 1in (2·5cm) thick planks of wood. It consists simply of a box complete with base, which should have plenty of drainage holes drilled in it.

A good depth for any planter is 18-24in (45-60cm). This will give plants a deep root run, and the compost will not dry out rapidly in hot weather. Planters are highly recommended for basement gardens and perhaps very small backyards, particularly if there is no natural soil.

As with tubs, planters should ideally be raised a few inches above the ground to allow excess water to drain away easily. If the planter is in close contact with the ground, a seal consisting of soil particles and algae is likely to form around the bottom edges, so impeding the drainage.

Above: *This gravel area at a front entrance has been brightened up with summer bedding plants in wooden and terracotta tubs and other ornamental containers.*

BARRELS

Full-size barrels can be used for all kinds of plants, but are most often used with planting holes in the sides, when they are popularly known as 'strawberry barrels' (see pp. 28-9).

If barrels are used without planting holes in the sides—in other words, if you simply plant subjects in the top—then the plants may look rather out of proportion in relation to the height of the container. If you want to use a barrel in this way, then the best choice of plants would be trailing species such as petunias, nasturtiums, lobelias, pendulous fuchsias, ivyleaf pelargoniums and trailing verbena.

An ideal, cheap, but short-term, container for growing vegetables on a patio, balcony or terrace is the growing-bag. These bags can also be used for summer bedding plants—especially on a balcony or roof garden where a light-weight container is preferable.

TYPES OF BAGS

Growing-bags are long, narrow polythene bags filled with soilless compost and available from a variety of manufacturers. The average length is 4ft (1·2m) but smaller ones are also available.

In the most up-to-date version, the compost comes in the form of a dehydrated compressed slab, easily transported. Once the bag is set in place, water is added and the slab swells up to fill the bag with compost.

Most growing-bags are not very attractive, coming in gaudy colours and covered with lettering —the name of the manufacturer and the brand name. Some,

however, are plain brown, and others are stone coloured to match the patio surface. If you wish to disguise the growing-bag completely, surround it with a line of bricks and cover the bag's surface with aggregate.

Extremely good plant growth is possible in growing-bags, provided the plants are fed regularly once they are well established. Bags do not dry out as quickly as pots.

PLANTING AND MANAGEMENT

Growing-bags must be placed on a firm, level surface. Then, following the manufacturer's instructions, a hole is cut in the top for each individual plant.

Apart from this, there are no special planting techniques. However, as the compost is soil-less, remember to firm it only very lightly when planting.

A 4ft (1·2m) long bag comfortably holds three to four tomato, capsicum or aubergine plants,

or two melon/cucumber plants.

The manufacturers usually recommend that you do not make drainage holes in the bottom of the bag, so water with care or the compost may become saturated. One manufacturer, however, does recommend drainage holes in the base, and these are marked on the bag. If, with ordinary bags, you find that heavy rain is making the compost too wet, then it is sensible to cut some drainage holes in the bottom. To prevent problems from drips if the bags are on a balcony or roof garden, stand them on shallow trays containing gravel.

To support tall crops, such as tomatoes, use proprietary growing-bag crop supports. Generally these are made from plastic-coated steel, and have special 'feet' which are placed under the bag. The weight of the bag then supports the frame.

It is not possible to use bamboo canes for supporting plants as there is insufficient depth of

compost to anchor them. Another way to support tall plants is to place the bag against a wall and to tie in the plants to trellis-work or horizontal wires fixed to the wall.

The plants will quickly use up all the fertilizer in the compost, so it is important to feed them regularly once they are established and growing steadily. About once a week is recommended. Most people will prefer to use a liquid fertilizer—choose a compound type containing nitrogen, phosphorus and potash, plus trace elements. You could use a tomato fertilizer for vegetables like capsicums and aubergines (and, of course, for tomatoes).

Never apply liquid fertilizer if the compost is dry and the plants are suffering from lack of moisture. Water them first, and then wait until they are fully charged with water before applying the fertilizer.

TYPES OF PLANTS

Many short-term plants can be grown in bags. The bags are not generally re-used, though, and it is best to buy new ones each year. You can, however, successfully grow a crop of winter lettuces after tomatoes, capsicums and so on. Spring bulbs could also be planted after these summer vegetables. But do not use the bags any more than this—after this second crop throw them away, or use the contents as a mulch somewhere in the garden.

Many small vegetables can be grown in bags, but not the long-rooted kinds, such as parsnips, leeks, or long beetroots, for example. Short-rooted root vegetables, though, will succeed. Examples include turnips, globe beetroots and stump-rooted and round-rooted carrots. Bags are also ideal for salad vegetables, such as lettuces, endive, spring onions and radishes. Herbs can be grown, too, as can strawberries.

Above: *Growing-bags can be placed on gravel trays to prevent drips, especially on balconies.*
Left: *Melons are suitable for growing-bag cultivation but should be in a warm sheltered spot.*

27

STRAWBERRY BARRELS AND BASKETS

Strawberry barrels allow many plants to be grown in a limited space, and can be very useful in town and city gardens, while hanging baskets ensure good use is made of otherwise wasted vertical wall space.

STRAWBERRY BARRELS

These are not difficult to make and can be constructed quite easily at home. Obtain a used, full-sized barrel and drill 2in (5cm) diameter holes in the sides, about 8in (20cm) apart, staggering them across the face of the barrel. Alternatively, proprietary PVC strawberry tubs are available.

The roots of the plants are pushed through the holes as the barrel is filled with compost, finishing with four plants in the top of the barrel.

Use such a barrel not only for strawberries but also for alpines like aubrieta, alyssum, saxifrages and sempervivums. It is also suitable for bedding plants, such as petunias, lobelia, mimulus and impatiens.

PARSLEY AND TOWER POTS

Parsley pots are similar in principle to the strawberry barrel, but smaller, generally about 12-16in (30-40cm) high. They are usually jar-shaped and made of terracotta clay, which may be natural or glazed.

Do not use them only for parsley, though: try other small herbs, trailing bedding plants and alpines.

A tower pot is a proprietary product designed for strawberries, but also useful for other plants. Basically it consists of a tall cylinder with planting 'pockets' protruding from the sides.

HANGING BASKETS

The traditional basket is made from galvanized wire; more modern varieties are plastic-coated, and both hang from

Above: *A basket of ivy-leaf pelargoniums and helichrysum.*
Below: *Fruitful use of a tower pot—luscious strawberries.*

chains. Another type is the solid plastic basket with built-in drip tray, hung from a chain or a plastic hanger. Colours include green, white, brown, black and terracotta. Some versions have a built-in water reservoir inside.

Large baskets have a diameter of 12-18in (30-45cm); small ones measure about 8in (20cm). Depth

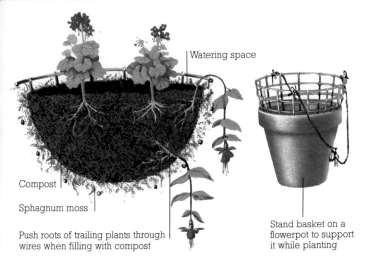

Watering space

Compost

Sphagnum moss

Push roots of trailing plants through wires when filling with compost

Stand basket on a flowerpot to support it while planting

Above: *Wire hanging baskets are a good choice as plants can be inserted around the sides, creating a 'ball' of colour.*

varies from 6 to 9in (15 to 23cm).

Wall-mounted baskets are also popular, and may be solid plastic or wire. There are many hanging pots available, too, in plastic or terracotta clay.

Filling and planting: Wire baskets are first lined with sphagnum moss, proprietary liners of various materials, or polythene sheeting with drainage holes.

Solid baskets are simply filled with compost and plants arranged in the top: upright plants in the centre and trailers around the edge. Either lightweight soilless composts can be used, or the soil-based type.

To give a 'ball' of colour with a wire basket, trailing plants can be planted through the wires as the basket is being filled with compost. At the top, again use upright plants in the centre with trailers around the edge. Leave a watering space at the top of about 1in (2·5cm). Water the plants in well after planting.

General care: Check baskets daily for water requirements as they dry out rapidly in hot weather. Once plants are well established

and coming into flower, feed weekly with a compound liquid fertilizer. This is essential, since the frequency of watering washes the nutrients out of the compost before they have all been absorbed by the roots.

PLANTS FOR BASKETS

Hanging baskets and similar containers are generally used for half-hardy annuals and perennials (summer bedding plants). However, there are a few suitable hardy plants to enable you to use some baskets all the year round.

Trailing plants: Ageratum, alyssum, aubrieta (hardy), begonia (pendulous tuberous types), *Campanula isophylla,* chlorophytum, fuchsia (trailing varieties), hedera (hardy), *Helichrysum petiolatum,* lobelia, nasturtium, pelargonium (ivy-leaved), petunia, tradescantia, verbena (trailing varieties), and *Vinca major* or *minor* varieties (hardy).

Upright plants: Begonia (tuberous and fibrous rooted), cineraria (silver foliage type), coleus, fuchsia (bush varieties), heliotrope, impatiens (also used as trailers), iresine, marigolds (French), mimulus (also used as trailers), and pelargonium (zonal).

29

SINK AND WATER GARDENS

A large container can be used to make a small self-contained garden, featuring a variety of plants in a miniaturized landscape. Such features will enhance any small garden, but are ideal for the patio. Likewise, a small self-contained water garden is easy to make and provides an attractive garden feature.

A SINK GARDEN

Old stone sinks are superb containers for alpines or rock plants on a sunny patio. Unfortunately they are now highly prized and difficult to obtain. The alternative is to acquire an old discarded glazed sink and to cover it with hypertufa.
Preparation: First 'paint' the outside, and several inches down the inside, with a waterproof bonding agent, as used by builders. When this is tacky, you can apply a layer of hypertufa. A hypertufa mix consists of 2 parts sphagnum peat, 1 part sand and 1 part cement (parts by volume). Add sufficient water to make a stiff but pliable mix.

Spread a layer about ½in (12mm) thick and create a rough textured surface to resemble natural stone. Leave to harden for two weeks before planting.
Filling: Place a large piece of broken clay flower pot (crock) over the drainage hole, making sure that the crock will still allow excess water to drain away. Next, add a layer of broken clay pots about 1in (2·5cm) deep. Top this with a thin layer of rough peat or leafmould.

Fill to within 1in (2·5cm) of the top with compost—John Innes potting compost No. 1, to which has been added one-third extra of coarse horticultural sand.
Planting: Start by planting one or two dwarf conifers, the most suitable for sink gardens being *Juniperus communis* 'Compressa'. Then other alpines can be added —plant some trailing kinds at the edges. Finally, spread a layer

of stone chippings over the compost about ½in (12mm) deep.

PLANTS FOR A SINK GARDEN

Aethionema armenum, pink flowers in June, 8in (20cm) spread. *Armeria caespitosa*, pink flowers, May, 6in (15cm) spread. *Dianthus neglectus*, rose-pink, June, 6in (15cm) spread. *Geranium cinereum*, pink, May, 6in (15cm) spread. *Gysophila caucasica*, white, June, 4in (10cm) spread. *Phlox douglasii*, lilac, May, 8in (20cm) spread. *Raoulia australis*, silvery foliage, low mats, 8in (20cm) spread. *Saxifraga* x *burseriana*, white, May, 6in (15cm) spread. *Sempervivum arachnoideum*, foliage covered with white webbing, 6in (15cm) spread.

HYPERTUFA ROCKS

Another way of growing alpines is in artificial rocks made of hypertufa mix. Use the same formula as before, but shovel the mix into a hole lined with pieces of rock. Leave the mix in the ground for a couple of weeks, then remove the hardened hypertufa and take out the rocks. Plant alpines in the holes, in compost as used for sink gardens.

Below: *Sinks make ideal containers for alpines or rock plants, including dwarf conifers. They are best placed on a patio in full sun to ensure good plant gowth.*

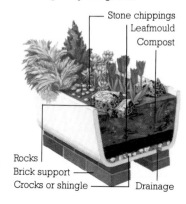

Stone chippings
Leafmould
Compost
Rocks
Brick support
Crocks or shingle
Drainage

A WATER GARDEN

A miniature water garden can be created in a wooden tub. If the tub leaks, line it with a piece of black butyl-rubber pool liner. Place the tub in a sunny spot on the patio. If preferred it may, instead, be sunk almost up to its rim elsewhere in the garden, with its edges surrounded by rocks and moisture-loving plants.

Below: *Containers for miniature water gardens can be sunk to the rim, and the edges 'land-scaped' with attractive rocks and small perennial plants.*

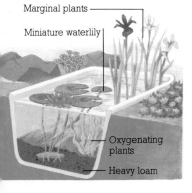

Marginal plants

Miniature waterlily

Oxygenating plants

Heavy loam

Above: *The white glazing of this sink makes a superb background for brightly coloured begonias, lobelia and pelargoniums.*

Place a layer of heavy loam in the bottom, between 4 and 6in (10 and 15cm) deep, and mound some up the sides in which to bed marginal plants. Plant a miniature waterlily in the middle, some oxygenating 'water weeds' and a few marginal plants around the sides. Finish with a layer of pea shingle to hold the soil in place.

AQUATICS FOR TUBS

Miniature waterlilies: *Nymphaea pygmaea alba,* white flowers; *N. pygmaea* 'Johann Pring', deep pink; and *N. pygmaea helvola,* soft yellow.
Oxygenating plants: water milfoil, species of myriophyllum.
Marginal plants: *Acorus gramineus variegatus,* yellow-striped, rush-like leaves; *Caltha palustris* 'Plena', yellow flowers, spring; *Menyanthes trifoliata,* bog bean, pink flowers; and *Sagittaria sagittifolia flore-pleno,* arrowhead, double white flowers.

31

DOUBLE WALLS AND RAISED BEDS

Walls and beds are perfect for creating variations in height in small backyards, basements and on patios, and they give great scope for imaginative planting schemes.

DOUBLE WALLS

These are not only decorative features but are designed for planting. A double wall can be built around or in front of a patio, terrace or porch, or it can be used as a front boundary wall. It would also make an attractive retaining wall for a terrace.

Do not worry whether it is in sun or shade for there are plants to suit both situations.

Construction: The best width for a double wall is usually 2-2½ft (60-75cm). Build each wall on a foundation of rammed rubble or hardcore topped with concrete —as shown in the drawing. Use bricks, ornamental concrete walling blocks or stone walling blocks, bedding them on mortar. With a drystone wall the joints are not mortared.

Filling and planting: Place a layer of rubble in the bottom for drainage and fill up with light to medium topsoil or with John Innes potting compost No. 2 or 3 (more expensive). Leave space for watering at the top.

With a drystone wall, trailing plants can be grown in the sides, with the roots in the compost. These can be planted as building progresses, or planting holes can be left between the walling stones and the plants inserted later.

PLANTS FOR DOUBLE WALLS

Rock plants: Alyssum, arabis, aubrieta (trailing), campanula (some trailing), dianthus, helianthemum, iberis, lewisia (plant in sides of drystone wall), sempervivums (plant in sides of drystone wall), and creeping thymes.

Miniature shrubs: Berberis (dwarf); cytisus (prostrate); daphne (dwarf); genista (dwarf); roses (miniature).

Conifers: *Chamaecyparis lawsoniana* 'Minima Aurea'; *C. obtusa* 'Nana'; *Juniperus communis* 'Compressa', prostrate juniper species; *Picea glauca* 'Albertiana Conica'; and *Pinus sylvestris* 'Beuvronensis'.

Perennials: *Achillea clypeolata; Anthemis cupaniana;* asters (dwarf); aquilegia (dwarf); cent-

Below: *Double walls for planting make an attractive surround for a patio, terrace or porch. This contains tulips and aubrieta.*

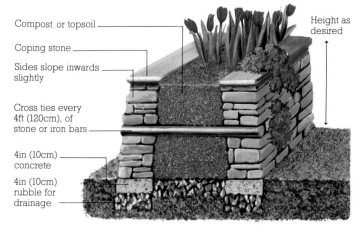

Compost or topsoil

Coping stone

Sides slope inwards slightly

Cross ties every 4ft (120cm), of stone or iron bars

4in (10cm) concrete

4in (10cm) rubble for drainage

Height as desired

ranthus (ideal for sides of drystone wall); *Euphorbia mysinites; Oenothera missouriensis;* potentilla hybrids; sedums; sisyrinchium; veronica (dwarf species); and *Zauschneria californica.*

Dwarf bulbs: Most dwarf bulbs will enjoy the good drainage, including tulip species, crocus species and alliums (dwarf).

RAISED BEDS

Raised beds can be built against walls or they may be free-standing. You can also build them on a patio, as this is a good foundation if properly laid. Site the bed either in sun or shade and then choose plants accordingly.

Construction: Beds can be made to any shape you desire—square, rectangular, round, and so on. The depth needs to be about 18-24in (45·5-60cm), and make sure you leave drainage holes in the sides at ground level.

Beds can be built up from bricks, ornamental concrete walling blocks, building blocks (including the lightweight kinds), logs, railway sleepers (timber), or natural stone (the latter can

Below: *With raised beds, potential planting schemes are limited only by your imagination. Here impatiens and white petunias flourish.*

be used as drystone walling).

Filling and planting: Place a layer of rubble or shingle in the bottom for drainage and fill with good light to medium topsoil. Alternatively, use John Innes potting compost No. 2 or 3. Remember to leave space for watering.

If you wish to grow limehating plants, use an acid topsoil or compost containing plenty of peat or leafmould. If you are growing mainly alpines and dwarf bulbs, use a very well-drained, gritty compost, like John Innes potting compost No. 2, to which has been added one-third extra of horti-cultural coarse sand or grit.

PLANTS FOR RAISED BEDS

Shrubs for lime-free beds: *Acer palmatum* varieties; calluna; cassiope; camellias; daboecia; erica; kalmia; pernettya; pieris and dwarf rhododendrons.

Perennials for lime-free beds: *Cornus canadensis;* lithospermum; meconopsis; pachysandra; some primulas; and tricyrtis.

For neutral or alkaline beds: There is a very wide range of small to medium-sized shrubs. Perennials of many kinds are suitable, as are bulbs, grasses, roses, small conifers and climbers. Avoid rampant spreaders.

COMPOSTS

Choosing a suitable compost can make all the difference between plants thriving and languishing. Newcomers can buy ready-mixed composts but more experienced or adventurous gardeners might like to mix their own—it is certainly cheaper.

SOIL-BASED OR SOILLESS?

Basically there are two types of compost for use in containers—soil-based, which consist of loam (soil), peat and sand, plus fertilizers (the traditional John Innes mixes), or the more modern, soilless composts, made up of peat, plus sand, vermiculite or perlite, and of course fertilizers.

Each has good and bad points. The points in favour of soilless composts are that they are light in weight and ideal for humus-loving plants, such as camellias. When used correctly, soilless composts encourage good root development and thus better plant growth.

On the negative side, soilless composts must be firmed lightly and may not be able to support large or heavy plants. Fertilizers are washed out of soilless composts comparatively quickly, which means more regular feeding. They are also difficult to moisten again once they have dried right out, and if watering is too frequent they will become saturated.

Soil-based composts, on the other hand, are heavy and ideal for large plants. Drainage and aeration are excellent if suitable materials have been used, and they are able to hold on to foods for much longer, so plants require less feeding. They are easily moistened if they dry out, and there is less likelihood of the gardener saturating the compost. They are, therefore, highly recommended for all plants, such as alpines, that like really well-drained and aerated composts.

Not all proprietary soil-based composts, however, have all of these good qualities. If very heavy

Top: *Compost for containers can be made from loam (well sifted), peat and sand, plus fertilizer.*
Above: *All ingredients must be thoroughly mixed, by turning the heap several times.*

loam or soil has been used, the compost will be poorly drained and aerated, and so will end up as a soggy, compact mass in the container. If you mix your own soil-based compost, you may have difficulty buying top-quality loam.

You have a choice of buying composts in bags from a garden centre, or mixing your own. The latter works out cheaper. Remember that if you are growing lime-hating plants such as camellias, azaleas and rhododendrons, you must use an acid or lime-free compost (often sold as ericaceous compost).

HOME-MADE JOHN INNES (J.I.) COMPOSTS

John Innes compost is basically a mixture of loam, peat and sand. You will need a bag of light or medium loam, partially sterilized, and with a pH of 6-6·5 (slightly acid). Pass it through a ⅜in (9mm) sieve before use. You will also need granulated moss peat, which has been passed through a ⅜in (9mm) sieve and moistened before mixing. The sand should be a lime-free sharp horticultural type, with 60-70 per cent of the particles between ¹⁄₁₆ and ⅛ (1·5 and 3mm) in diameter. Mix the compost by the bushel (8 gallons or 36 litres), using a one-gallon bucket.

J.I. seed compost
Used mainly for seed sowing.
- 2 parts loam
- 1 part peat
- 1 part sand
  (all throughly mixed)
  To each bushel add
- 1½oz (42g) superphosphate
- ¾oz (21g) chalk or ground limestone.

J.I. potting composts (J.I.P.)
Use No. 1 for initial potting of young plants, No. 2 for potting on, and No. 3 for plants that like a rich compost or for large plants.

J.I.P. 1
- 7 parts loam
- 3 parts peat
- 2 parts sand
  (all thoroughly mixed)
  To each bushel of this mix add
- 4oz (113g) John Innes base fertiliser (obtainable from garden centres)
- ¾oz (21g) chalk or ground limestone.

J.I.P. 2
Basic mix as above, but add per bushel
- 8oz (226g) J.I. base
- 1½oz (42g) chalk or ground limestone.

J.I.P. 3
Basic mix as above, but add per bushel
- 12oz (340g) J.I. base
- 2¼oz (63g) chalk or ground limestone.

HOME-MADE SOILLESS COMPOSTS

Seed compost
- 1 part peat
- 1 part sand (or use the lighter materials perlite or vermiculite instead of sand)
- Add, as directed by the makers, a proprietary, complete, seed compost fertilizer base.

Potting compost
- 3 parts peat
- 1 part sand (or perlite or vermiculite)
- Add, as directed by the makers, a proprietary potting compost fertilizer base.

COMPOST FOR CACTI AND ALPINES

Both of these are best grown in a very well-drained and aerated soil-based compost. J.I.P. 2, to which has been added one-third extra of sharp sand, is recommended. Proprietary cactus composts are available if home-mixing is not practicable.

LIME-FREE COMPOSTS

If you are mixing your own, follow the formulae for the J.I. seed or potting mixtures, but use acid loam and omit the chalk or limestone.

For a soilless mix use the potting compost formula, but ideally with a little acid loam added, and some leafmould. With these ingredients, no fertilizer will be necessary.

COMPOSTS FOR CUTTINGS

There are a variety of suitable composts for cuttings, all easy to make:
- Equal parts peat and sand
- Equal parts peat and perlite
- Equal parts peat and vermiculite
- Pure perlite or vermiculite
  No fertilizer is required for cutting composts.

TOOLS AND PLANT SUPPORTS

As with other forms of gardening, it is surprising how much equipment is needed even when activities are confined to containers on a patio, balcony or roof garden. But virtually all the items described here are considered essential.

TOOLS

Gardening knife: This is extremely useful for tasks such as dead-heading, general trimming and for taking cuttings. Buy a general-purpose type of the highest possible quality—it should then last many years and the blade will stay keen without frequent sharpening. Avoid a stainless-steel blade as it is difficult to obtain a really sharp edge.

Secateurs: Essential for pruning all kinds of plants. Again go for top quality and ideally the parrot-bill rather than the anvil type. Designs range from lightweight (ideal for dead-heading, cutting down herbaceous plants, etc.) to heavy-duty (for pruning shrubs and trees).

Shears: Again, go for high-quality steel. Shears are used for trimming hedges, lightly trimming such plants as heathers, and for trimming lawn edges or awkward parts of the lawn.

Hand fork and trowel: Stainless-steel forks and trowels are a joy to use if you can afford them. A hand fork is useful for pricking over the soil surface and for forking out weeds. A hand trowel is useful for planting small plants.

Bucket or trug: These are handy containers for rubbish when you are tidying up, dead-heading and weeding.

Garden compost container: All soft garden rubbish goes into this to rot down into garden compost. Many proprietary containers are available, but it is quite easy to make your own.

Incinerator: Useful in the garden for burning woody rubbish, such as shrub prunings. A steel-mesh type can be recommended.

Above: *White plastic-coated steel trellis makes an attractive support for this firethorn or pyrancantha, and many other plants, too.*

Yard broom: A stiff broom will be needed for sweeping the patio and paths and for scrubbing them down to remove dirt.

Watering can: This is needed for watering containers. Most are plastic these days and light in weight. A long spout is useful for watering hanging baskets and other elevated containers. Buy a selection of roses, from fine to coarse, for watering seedlings and young, delicate plants.

Hosepipe: Useful for quickly watering many containers, especially if fitted with a watering lance with an on/off trigger. This will also enable you to water

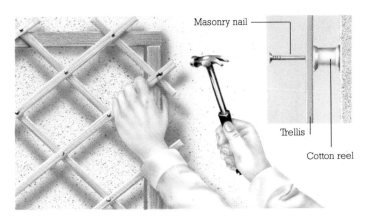

Masonry nail

Trellis

Cotton reel

Above left: *Trellis should be held away from a wall to ensure good air circulation. One way of doing this is to use cotton reels as spacers (above right).*
Left: *Most climbers should be tied in with soft garden string.*

hanging baskets easily. A hose reel will keep the hosepipe tidy when not in use.
Pesticide sprayer: Buy a small pressure sprayer for applying insecticides and fungicides. Reasonably priced plastic models are available.

SUPPORTS FOR CLIMBERS

Trellis: Panels of trellis can be fixed about 2in (5cm) away from the wall to support climbers. There is a choice of trellis—wood, plastic-coated steel and strong plastic. The former will need regular treatment with a horti-cultural wood preservative; the others are maintenance-free and are available in various colours, such as green or white. Large wooden trellis panels are ideal

for forming free-standing screens.
Horizontal wires: Heavy-gauge galvanised or plastic-coated wires spaced 12in (30cm) apart on a wall or fence make suitable sup-ports for climbers. Support them with 'vine eyes'—these are available to suit masonry or timber. If you want the wires to be really tight use straining bolts to attach each end.
Wall or masonry nails: These can be hammered into a wall to support wires, or plants can be tied to their protruding heads.
Bamboo canes: Various lengths and thicknesses are available for supporting such plants as herbaceous perennials, tomatoes, etc. Cedarwood stakes are used for heavier plants, such as tall, newly planted shrubs.
Link-stakes: These are proprie-tary products consisting of metal supports that can be linked together to encircle and support completely such plants as herbaceous perennials.
Tying materials: The most widely used are soft green garden string and raffia. For long-term ties, use tarred string.

37

FLOORING MATERIALS AND DESIGNS

There is an extremely wide range of flooring materials available for constructing patios, terraces and courtyards. They should ideally harmonize with the style of the house and the rest of the garden —or pleasantly contrast with them.

CONCRETE

Concrete makes a good patio surface for the modern house. To avoid excessive glare, which sometimes occurs in bright weather, the concrete can be coloured by mixing in proprietary colouring powders. For a textured surface, lightly brush the surface of the concrete while it is still wet. This will expose the aggregate.

A suitable concrete mix consists of 1 part cement, 2 parts sand and 3 parts aggregate/shingle. Mix with 1 part water and lay it 3in (7·5cm) thick.

Above: *Several materials can be used together to create an interesting surface.*

BRICKS

Areas of brick look very attractive in informal or cottage gardens, particularly old bricks, but they can also be used to good effect around modern buildings. Use special hard paving bricks, or stock bricks.

Bricks can be laid in various patterns, such as basketweave or herringbone, or staggered like bricks in the house wall. They are best loosely laid. Lay them flat, rather than on edge, and leave ⅜in (9mm) joints, which you can fill with sand.

TIMBER DECKING

This is low-level decking, raised a few inches off the ground and supported on wooden posts. It looks particularly good with modern houses. Decking more than 18in (45cm) off the ground should be fitted with a safety rail.

There are various kinds of suitable timber. Western red cedar or chestnut are excellent for outdoor use, but ordinary deal or pine can be used provided it is thoroughly treated with preservative. Use a brand incorporating a dark brown stain if preferred.

NATURAL STONE

Of the many kinds of natural stone, sandstone and limestone are the most popular for garden use. They are available as square paving slabs with a textured surface, and random stone slabs for use as 'crazy paving', in which fairly wide joints are created and filled with soil. Carpeting plants, such as creeping thymes, can then be planted in the paving joints.

Marble is attractive, but its cool appearance is more in keeping with warm climates. However, it

Below: *Shingle comes in various colours and can be used to create dramatic contrasts.*

can be recommended for small courtyards in city garden. For safety it should have a honed non-slip surface.

PAVING SLABS

Artificial slabs are ideal for modern houses. They are made from concrete and come in various sizes and shapes, such as square, rectangular or hexagonal. There are various textured surfaces available, too, often imitating natural stone, and most are non-slip.

Large expanses of paving can be 'broken up' with areas of other materials, such as granite setts, cobbles or gravel.

Quarry tiles, often heather coloured, can be used with virtually any style of building.

GRAVEL

Gravel looks good whether it is associated with modern buildings or with period architecture. Gravel areas are also pleasing when used with artificial paving slabs to provide a variation in texture.

Pea shingle is often used and should be spread no more than 1in (2·5cm) thick. Gravel may need confining by edging the area with partially buried wooden boards, or by a surround of bricks.

PREPARING FOUNDATIONS AND LAYING PAVING

The materials mentioned here should be laid on solid foundations, consisting of 4in (10cm) of well-rammed hardcore, placed on level, consolidated soil. Top with 1½in (4cm) of soft builders' sand to create a smooth, level bed for the surfacing material. Gravel, however, is best laid on the top of well-consolidated soil.

Slabs, paving stones, and similar materials can be spot bedded on mortar—five dabs of mortar per slab. Gently tap down level and leave ¼in (6mm) joints, which you later grout with mortar.

FILLING AND PLANTING CONTAINERS

Don't rush planting—take your time and make a really good job of it. Ensure the containers drain properly, since this helps plants establish quickly. Many plants are in containers for a long time, so mistakes made during planting are not easily rectified.

PREPARING A CONTAINER

First make sure there are drainage holes in the bottom. These must not clog up with soil, so cover them with a layer of drainage material, about 1in (2·5cm) deep. Pots under 6in (15cm) in diameter may not need drainage material.

The best type of drainage material consists of broken clay flower pots, known as 'crocks'. Bridge large pieces over the drainage holes and top up with smaller crocks. Add a fibrous layer, again about 1in (2·5cm) deep, to prevent compost from washing down into the crocks and blocking them. Rough peat, leaf-mould and turf fibre are ideal.

If the plant is dry stand the root-ball in a bucket of water for an hour or until no more bubbles rise to the surface. This will thoroughly wet the compost. Allow it to drain before planting.

Place a layer of compost in the bottom of the container, of sufficient depth so that when planting is completed, the top of the plant's rootball is ½in (12mm) below the level of the new compost. Allow also sufficient space for watering at the top—from ½ to 1in (12mm to 2·5cm), depending on the size of container. Firm the compost moderately if soil-based, lightly if soilless.

PLANTING

Most plants available today are sold in pots or other kinds of container. Carefully remove the plant from its nursery container to avoid root disturbance. If it is in a rigid pot, invert the plant, tap the rim of the pot on a solid surface and slide the rootball out. If it is in a black plastic bag, carefully slit this down one side and underneath with a knife and peel it away from the rootball.

Place the plant centrally in the container and, at this stage, adjust

Above: *Put plenty of drainage material in containers when planting bulbs and other plants. Broken clay pots are used here.*

Above: *Bulbs, such as these tulips, should be spaced out so that they are not quite touching each other.*

the depth of the bottom compost layer if necessary.

Now trickle compost between the rootball and the sides of the container, firming it with your fingers as you proceed—again moderately firm for soil-based composts, or very lightly for soilless types. Always try to match the degree of compaction of the rootball, if possible. This will encourage the roots to penetrate their new surroundings.

Of course, not all plants will be in pots—some may be bare-rooted, with the roots wrapped in, say, polythene or hessian. This may apply to certain shrubs, trees and fruit trees, and also to summer bedding plants if they were raised in trays.

When planting bare-rooted specimens, make sure their roots are well spread out, and also allow them to dangle well down in the container. Hold the plant in the desired position and trickle compost between and around the roots, firming as you proceed. Initially you can gently shake the plant up and down to make sure the compost is worked well

Above: *To remove a young plant from a pot, invert it, tap the rim on the edge of a bench, and carefully slide out the rootball.*

between the roots. All the time, you are trying to avoid air pockets around the root system.

Bare-rooted plants should be planted to the same depth—with trees and shrubs this is indicated by a soil mark at the stem base.

If bare-rooted plants have very long roots, there is no harm in reducing them in length before planting—by up to one-third. Dead roots must be completely removed, and if any are damaged they must be cut off. Always use very sharp secateurs.

AFTERCARE

Immediately after planting, thoroughly water in, applying sufficient so that excess water runs out of the bottom of the container. This helps to settle the compost around the roots, which is especially necessary when using soilless composts.

It may be necessary to cut some plants back after planting—especially certain deciduous shrubs and climbers such as grape vines, clematis, and roses planted in the dormant season.

Above: *Once bulbs have been set in place, trickle compost between them and firm it lightly. Leave watering space at the top.*

WATERING

Watering causes more problems for those new to gardening than any other aspect of plant care. When do plants need watering? How much water should be applied? These are the most commonly asked questions.

HOW AND WHEN TO WATER

Do not wait until a plant wilts before watering. By this stage, damage has already been done and plant growth checked. With evergreens, such as conifers and camellias, the leaves and flower buds may drop if the compost is allowed to dry out completely.

There are some simple tests you can carry out to decide whether or not a plant needs watering. The first is the finger test. Push your finger down into the top ½in (12mm) or so of compost. If it feels dry at the top of the container, then it is safe to apply water. If it is wet, then leave well alone—further water could result in saturated compost, and the plant will suffer.

Another indication that water is needed is when the compost changes surface colour. When it is dark it is generally wet enough, but as it dries out it turns a lighter colour, indicating that water is needed.

Weight is also a guide. If smaller pots can be lifted, they will be much heavier when the compost is wet, than when it is dry.

If you do not want to rely on your own judgement—and it should be said that this comes with experience—then use one of the proprietary soil-moisture meters. These meters have probes which are pushed down into the compost. Most meters are marked 'dry', 'moist' and 'wet'.

If you decide that a plant needs watering then you must water heavily—it is no use just giving a quick 'splash', since this will only wet the surface of the compost where there is, generally, little of the root system. Apply sufficient water to wet the compost right

Above: *It is essential to check hanging baskets once or twice a day as the compost can dry out rapidly in warm weather.*

the way through, so that it actually runs out of the bottom. This means filling the entire space between the compost surface and the rim of the container, pouring the water on fairly quickly.

After watering leave well alone until the compost is starting to dry out again. You could kill plants if you water them every day regardless of whether it is needed or not.

The rate of drying out depends on the time of year and the weather. Obviously in hot summer weather, compost can dry out rapidly, so it is not unknown for container plants to need watering twice a day! In cool or cold weather the compost dries out much more slowly. Indeed, it is possible that in winter plants will not need additional watering.

WATERING EQUIPMENT

Most people will use a watering can for container plants. Choose one with a long spout if containers are not easy to reach, or you have hanging baskets to water.

If you have a lot of containers and decide to use a hosepipe, fit this with a spray nozzle (the type that you can regulate) or, even better, a watering lance with an on/off trigger. This is ideal for controlled watering of potted plants and hanging baskets.

Drip irrigation (the spaghetti system) is useful if you are unable to attend to your plants regularly, for it will water them automatically. Such a system can be fed from a reservoir bag, or from the mains water supply via a header tank fitted with a ballcock valve. Use automatic watering only in spring and summer.

You may not want hanging baskets, window boxes and plants on balconies to drip. The answer here is to use drip trays (some baskets have built-in types). Do not allow the surplus water to remain in the trays, though, or the compost will become saturated.

Below: *Lime-hating plants like rhododendron (shown here) and camellias must be watered only with lime-free water, such as rainwater, or they may be killed.*

TYPE OF WATER

Your tap water will be either 'hard' (containing a lot of lime) or 'soft' (containing little or no lime). The vast majority of plants can be safely watered with hard tapwater.

However, lime-hating plants, like rhododendrons and camellias, must on no account be watered with hard water, for they will suffer from an excess of lime—the leaves will turn yellow and the plants will be stunted. If your tapwater is soft you will have no problem, but if it is hard or alkaline then you will have to collect rainwater in a butt and reserve this for your lime-haters.

It is best to use water at the same temperature as the atmosphere if possible, and this means, again, storing water in a butt. But if this is not practicable then do not be too concerned.

FEEDING

Composts do not contain an inexhaustible supply of plant food, and once plants are well established in their containers, regular feeding will be required in the spring and summer.

NUTRIENTS NEEDED

All plants need the major nutrients nitrogen, phosphorus and potash. Nitrogen is responsible for vegetative growth—the stems and leaves. Phosphorus helps growth in various ways but it is important for healthy root development—seedlings and young plants, especially, need a supply of phosphorus. Potash is responsible for flowering and fruiting.

There are many other nutrients needed in smaller quantities, and these are known as trace elements. Particularly important are magnesium, manganese and iron, which are often included in compound fertilizers.

THE FEEDING PERIOD

Fertilizers are only applied in the growing season—spring, summer and perhaps early autumn. Start feeding plants only when they are well-established in their containers—about eight weeks after planting or potting on. Don't feed in winter as the food will not be used by the plants: it will build up in the compost and damage the roots. As a general rule, established plants are fed once a fortnight in the growing period, but plants which have completely filled their containers may need weekly feeding.

COMPOUND FERTILIZERS

Most gardeners will apply compound fertilizers, which supply nitrogen (N), phosphorus (P) and potash (K), plus perhaps trace elements. Compound fertilizers may be granular or liquid. The former are simply sprinkled on the compost surface and lightly forked in. The liquids are diluted with water and watered on to the compost. The well-known Growmore is a compound fertilizer with an analysis of 7 per cent N, 7 per cent P and 7 per cent K. It is sold in liquid or granular form.

Some compound fertilizers contain more potash, and are

Above: *Granular or powdered compound fertilizers are lightly sprinkled over the surface of the compost for established plants.*

Above: *Although not essential, it does speed the release of foods if dry compound fertilizers are lightly pricked into the surface.*

44

especially useful for flowering and fruiting plants. One well-known brand has an analysis of 10 per cent N, 10 per cent P and 27 per cent K. Tomato fertilizer is useful, too, for ornamentals and a typical analysis is 4 per cent N, 4 per cent P and 7 per cent K.

SINGLE FERTILIZERS

These contain only one plant food and can be useful if you want to boost the plants—say with nitrogen to encourage better stem and leaf growth. Sulphate of ammonia supplies nitrogen (21 per cent), superphosphate supplies phosphorus (18 per cent) and sulphate of potash provides potash (48 per cent).

TABLETS AND SPIKES

An old method of applying fertilizer, which has recently been revived, is fertilizer tablets. These supply nitrogen, phosphorus and potash, plus essential trace elements. They are simply pushed into the compost where they release their foods slowly over several weeks, so cutting down

the time spent on feeding.

Fertilizer spikes are similar to tablets, but they are in the shape of a spike that can be easily pushed into the compost.

FOLIAR FEEDING

This involves spraying the leaves with a liquid fertilizer, which is quickly absorbed and used by the plants. There are proprietary foliar fertilizers available and they are used on languishing plants to give them a quick boost. Foliar feeds must not be used as an alternative to applying compound fertilizer to the compost, but they are a useful source of nutrients.

TOP DRESSING

This involves replacing the top 1in (2·5cm) or so of the old compost with fresh material, and is usually carried out in the spring. It is an alternative to repotting or potting on, and is mainly used for large plants in final containers. Simply scrape off some of the old compost and replace with new, which will then supply food to the plant.

Above: *Fertilizer tablets are pushed into the compost where they release their foods slowly over several weeks.*

Above: *Fertilizer spikes work in the same way and are very easily pushed into the compost owing to their shape.*

GROOMING AND TRAINING

Plants really look their best when luxuriant and well shaped. Unfortunately this does not come about naturally with most plants, and so a vital part of the gardener's job involves grooming and training specimens. This process also helps to maintain a balance in the overall planting scheme.

DEAD FLOWERS AND FOLIAGE

Wherever possible dead flowerheads should be removed, unless they are to be followed by fruits or berries. There is no point in letting ornamental plants (which are grown for flowers only) set seeds, for this drains their energy. Indeed, removing dead blooms often encourages more to follow.

Plants which particularly benefit from this treatment include roses, camellias (some drop their dead blooms naturally), azaleas and fuchsias.

Hardy and half-hardy annuals should be regularly dead-headed, since this encourages a continuous display.

Another reason for removing dead blooms is that they can become infected with botrytis, or grey mould.

Above: Plants can be tied in with soft green garden string (left and bottom right) or with split rings (top right).

Above: Strong-growing plants, like some clematis, can be tied in to pergolas with strong nylon string, but not too tightly.

PINCHING OUT

Some young plants need the growing tips pinched out to encourage really bushy growth. This applies to some half-hardy annuals and perennials, such as fuchsias and heliotrope. Simply nip out the growing tip between finger and thumb, to produce plenty of new side shoots. Fuchsias benefit from having the side shoots pinched out, too. Other plants that are pinched out when small include chrysanthemums, dahlias and carnations.

TYING IN PLANTS

As they grow, climbers and other tall plants need tying in regularly to their supports. Tie in stems while they are still young and pliable, so that they can be trained into any desired position.

For tying in most plants, soft green garden string is a suitable material, looped in a figure of eight around the stem and the support. But if you want longer-lasting ties, then tarred string is the best to use.

46

Above: *Some plants, such as fuchsias, need their growing tips pinched out to encourage an attractive bushy habit of growth.*

Above: *Many climbers need tying in to wall trellis as they are not self-supporting—use soft garden string.*

Thin-stemmed plants, like carnations, can be tied in to canes with split wire plant rings, or with raffia. Twiggy hazel sticks, pushed into the compost among the plants, will support weak-stemmed annuals.

On no account tie in plants too tightly—leave sufficient space for stems to thicken. If a tie cuts into a stem it will seriously damage it and may prevent the flow of sap.

THINNING

To give better-quality growth and flowers, the removal of surplus shoots or stems that have become very overcrowded is recommended. For instance, dahlias often make a mass of stems and these are best thinned at an early stage of development.

Some permanent climbers like jasmine and Passion flower will become a tangled mass unless the older stems are thinned out in the winter or early spring, leaving young stems that can then be spaced out and tied in to suitable supports.

If you grow fruit trees you may need to thin the fruits to make sure the trees are not overloaded. With apples, for instance, the large fruit in the centre of the cluster, if sound, is allowed to remain and the smaller ones surrounding it removed. If it is malformed, remove it and thin the remainder to leave one or two of the best and healthiest. Bunches of grapes will need some of the berries removed to allow the rest to develop properly. Most of those in the centre are cut out, then the outside of the bunch is thinned.

REDUNDANT FLOWERS

Most plants which are grown mainly for their attractive foliage can be allowed to flower, but there are some that benefit from having their flower buds pinched out, mainly to prevent them becoming tall and lanky. This applies especially to coleus, which are often used for summer bedding, but don't allow silver-leaved cinerarias or golden pyrethrums to flower, either.

PRUNING

Contrary to popular belief, many shrubs, climbers and trees need no regular pruning. However, there are probably plenty on your patio or growing in containers that do, so take out your secateurs annually for the following.

ROSES

Large-flowered (hybrid teas): These are pruned in early spring. Strong stems are shortened by half to two-thirds of their length; weaker ones to 2-3in (5-7·5cm).

Cluster-flowered (floribundas): In early spring, strong stems are shortened by one-third to one half, weak ones by two-thirds.

Standards: Prune in early spring, but ensure all branches are the same length.

Climbers: Cut back side shoots to within one to three buds of the main stems in early spring.

Ramblers: Those which make new shoots near the base have their old flower stems cut right out immediately after flowering.

Miniatures: Little or no pruning is needed except for the removal of spent flowers and dead shoots.

General comments: Carry out dead heading regularly; remove dead, diseased and very weak shoots, retaining only strong

Above: *All shrubs should have dead wood regularly removed—it is often found on the inside and at the base of the plants.*

Below: *Large-flowered or hybrid tea roses are pruned hard annually in early spring to ensure really large blooms of good shape.*

Far right: *Rambler roses should have their old flower-bearing stems cut right out immediately after the plant has flowered— generally in early autumn.*

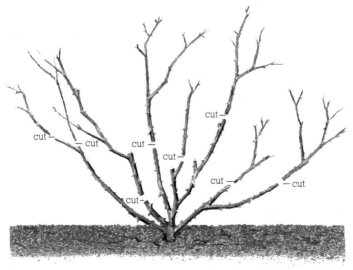

shoots; cut to outward-facing buds, just above the buds; and keep the centres of bush roses open.

CLIMBERS

Clematis: Check a plant's pruning needs when buying, as it is a complex subject. Prune early (spring) flowering kinds after flowering (*C. armandii, C. macropetala, C. montana* for example). Cut out completely some of the older stems. Large-flowered hybrids, which bloom in early summer, should be pruned in late winter. The previous year's shoots can be cut back a few inches to buds or new shoots. Those which flower in midsummer can be cut back to within 3ft (90cm) of the ground.
Jasmines: *Jasminum nudiflorum* is pruned after flowering by cutting back the flowered side shoots almost to the main stems. *J. officinale* should have the oldest stems cut out after flowering.
Wisteria: In midsummer, cut back side shoots to within 6in (15cm) of the main stems. In mid-winter shorten them to two buds.
Grape vines: Cut back side shoots in early winter to within two buds of the main stems.
General comments: With all climbers, thin out any weak or congested growth; tie in main stems regularly; space out main stems well.

SHRUBS

Deciduous shrubs that flower on shoots produced in previous years—for example, philadelphus, forsythia, weigela—should be pruned immediately after flowering by cutting back old flowered shoots to new ones lower down.

Deciduous shrubs that flower on the current year's shoots, and coloured-stemmed shrubs—for example, buddleias, cornus (dogwoods), fuchsias—should be pruned in early spring, almost down to soil level.

FORMALLY CLIPPED TREES

Bay, box, yew and holly, for example, are often grown as clipped specimens in tubs. Carry out clipping about once a month during the summer growing season to ensure dense growth and a neat appearance. Large-leaved kinds, such as bay and holly, are best clipped with secateurs; shears cut the leaves in half, which then go brown at the edges and look unsightly.

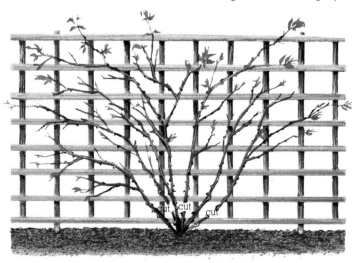

REPOTTING AND POTTING-ON

Permanent plants cannot remain in the same container indefinitely. As they fill their containers with roots they should be moved on to larger ones—this is known as potting-on. Plants already in large containers can be repotted into the same container, using fresh compost, to keep them growing and healthy.

HOW TO POT-ON

Plants should be potted-on before they outgrow their containers —certainly before the compost becomes tightly packed with roots, when the plant is said to be 'pot bound'. This condition will

Above: *Plants in large final containers, such as this yucca, benefit from repotting every two years to provide fresh compost.*

severely check the plant's growth.

Plants in large final containers benefit from repotting every two years or so, to give them a supply of fresh compost.

The best time for each of these operations is in the early spring just before growth commences. But young and temporary plants may need potting on in summer, too.

First, you must check root development. Invert the pot or container, tap the rim on a

hard surface, such as a bench, and slide out the rootball. If the compost is completely permeated with roots, then pot-on the plant. As a general rule, it is best to move plants on to the next size of container, or perhaps move them on two sizes. For instance, plants in 3in (7·5cm) pots are often moved to 5in (12·5cm) pots; plants in 6in (15cm) pots may be moved to 8in (20cm) pots.

What you should avoid is a big move, for no plant likes a large volume of compost around

Below: *Potting-on or repotting cacti need not be a thorny problem. Use a roll of newspaper to hold the plant. You can use a pruning glove, but this tends to be too cumbersome—you cannot get a really good grip on the plant.*

Above: *Removing a large plant from a container. While one person gently pulls, the other firmly taps the rim of the container.*

its roots. The plant will not immediately root into it all, and so there is a chance that the compost will remain wet. This could lead to root rot.

When potting-on plants use the technique described earlier in the book (see pages 40-41).

HOW TO REPOT

You may need some help if you are repotting a plant in a large container. In this instance, lay the container on its side. The other person should carefully, but firmly, hold the plant and gently pull it, while you tap the rim of the container with, say, a block of wood. This technique should allow the rootball to be slid out.

The next stage is to reduce the size of the rootball. Rub or tease away up to 2in (5cm) of soil from the base, sides and top of the rootball. Prune back the roots as well if necessary.

Next, wash the container to remove all soil adhering to it and allow the pot to dry before replanting, using fresh compost (see pages 40-41). As you are filling in with fresh compost, try to vibrate the plant to work the compost between the roots. Avoid leaving air spaces. After repotting, water heavily to settle the compost around the roots.

PROPAGATION

Many plants are easily raised from seeds, cuttings and division, which works out very much cheaper than buying large or flowering-size specimens. The scope for propagation is considerably widened if you have a greenhouse and a heated propagator.

SEEDS

Half-hardy annuals and perennials can be raised between late winter and mid-spring in a frost-free greenhouse. Suitable plants include pelargoniums, ageratum, marigolds, petunias, lobelia, salvias, alyssum, begonias, heliotrope, nicotiana and verbena.

They need to be raised in a propagator with a temperature of between 65° and 70°F (18° and 21°C). Transplant the seedlings into trays or small pots and grow in a heated greenhouse. Harden off in a cold frame and plant out in late spring.

In seed catalogues you will also find many shrubs, perennials and alpines that can be grown from seeds.

DIVISION

Herbaceous perennials and many alpines can be increased by division. In early spring lift clump-or mat-forming plants and carefully pull them apart to give smaller pieces complete with roots and buds (or top growth).

You may find that two long-handled hand forks, thrust back to back through the centre of a clump and gently levered apart, make division easier. Generally, you should discard the centre part of a clump and replant the young, vigorous outer portions.

Plants which can be divided include hostas, agapanthus, hemerocallis, and saxifrages.

SOFT OR TIP CUTTINGS

Many shrubs and perennials that produce soft, young side shoots or basal shoots, can be increased from these in spring.

Trim the cuttings to about 3in (7·5cm) in length, making the bottom cut immediately below a node or leaf joint. Remove lower leaves, dip the bases in hormone rooting powder and insert the cuttings up to the lower leaves in pots of cutting compost. Root in a heated propagator.

HALF-RIPE CUTTINGS

These are prepared in the same way as soft cuttings, but are taken later in the year—generally in late summer when the bases of the shoots are becoming hard or ripe. Many shrubs and conifers can be increased by

Below: *Many herbaceous perennials can be increased by dividing the clumps into a number of smaller portions in early spring.*

Discard centre of clump

Growth buds

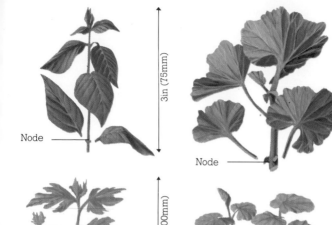

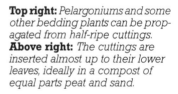

Node

3in (75mm)

3-4in (75-100mm)

2-4in (50-100mm)

Node

Cutting
compost

Top left: *Many shrubs can be propagated from cuttings of soft young side shoots in the spring.*
Above left: *Some perennials can be increased from soft shoots soon after they are produced in the spring, removing them low down.*

Top right: *Pelargoniums and some other bedding plants can be propagated from half-ripe cuttings.*
Above right: *The cuttings are inserted almost up to their lower leaves, ideally in a compost of equal parts peat and sand.*

this method, plus bedding plants such as pelargoniums. Again, the best results are achieved in a propagator, but half-ripe cuttings can also be rooted in a cold frame or under cloches.

wire bent to the shape of a hair-pin. They will root within a few weeks, and then you can cut the stem from the parent plant.

PLANTLETS

Some plants produce plantlets on the ends of stems, a well-known example being the spider plant, or chlorophytum, which is often used for summer display in containers and baskets.

These plantlets can be rooted in small pots of compost before they are detached from the parent plant. Pin them down into the compost with a piece of

BUYING-IN PLANTS

Shrubs, trees, climbers, coni-fers, herbaceous perennials, alpines and so on, which are sold in containers at garden centres, can be bought and planted at any time of year. Bare-root plants are bought and planted in the winter dormant season.

Half-hardy annuals and peren-nials are best purchased in late spring and planted in early summer, and kept in a cold frame until planting time.

53

PESTS AND DISEASES

Plants in containers are not troubled to the same extent by pests and diseases as plants in the rest of the garden. Certainly soil-borne troubles are not so common. If you grow plants well, they will be better able to withstand pests and will be less prone to diseases.

SPRAYING PLANTS

Suitable pesticides are recommended in the accompanying table. Use a garden pressure sprayer to wet all parts of the plants thoroughly—including the undersides of the leaves and the shoot tips.

Particularly recommended are the modern systemic pesticides, such as benomyl and dimethoate —these are absorbed by the plants and are not washed off by rain. They are also long-lasting.

BIRDS AND ANIMALS

Birds: Pigeons, sparrows, starlings and so on can damage plants by pecking at flowers, buds and leaves. Use a bird and animal deterrent based on aluminium ammonium sulphate, as directed by the maker.
Cats: These animals often scratch up soil—especially freshly-dug seed beds—and disturb plants. Again, use a bird and animal deterrent.
Mice: Seeds and bulbs often fall victim to the nocturnal activities of mice. Use a rat and mouse killer in pellet form, placing it near feeding sites or nests.

WEEDS

Weeds on patios, paths and gravel areas can be controlled using a path weedkiller containing paraquat, diquat, simazine and aminotriazole. This kills existing weeds and prevents weed seeds from germinating. Avoid contact with cultivated plants. Isolated plants can be spot treated using glyphosate in gel form.

Pests
Ants
Blackfly, greenfly
Capsid bugs
Caterpillars
Cutworms
Earwigs
Frog hoppers
Leaf hoppers
Leaf miner
Red spider mite
Scale insects
Thrips
Vine weevil
Whitefly
Woodlice

Diseases
Black spot
Botrytis (greymould)
Chlorosis
Leaf spots
Mildew
Rusts
Viruses

Symptoms	Control
Ant hills under plants, which wilt	Permethrin or gamma-HCH dust around nests
Bugs which suck sap of plants	Pirimicarb, dimethoate, pirimiphos-methyl, malathion
Puncture leaves and cause distortion	Gamma-HCH, dimethoate
Holes in leaves	Permethrin, derris dust, pirimiphos-methyl
Grubs eat roots and stems	Pirimiphos-methyl or diazinon dust around plants
Damage flowers	Gamma-HCH, trichlorphon
Bugs covered with white froth	Pirimiphos-methyl, malathion
Green insects causing leaf mottling	Pirimiphos-methyl
Leaves tunnelled	Pirimiphos-methyl, dimethoate
Fine pale mottling on leaves	Pirimiphos-methyl, dimethoate
Immobile brown scales on leaves and stems which suck the sap	Pirimiphos-methyl, malathion, dimethoate
White-mottled leaves and flowers	Pirimiphos-methyl, derris, malathion
Grubs eat the roots, adults eat leaf edges	Pirimiphos-methyl or gamma-HCH as soil drench
Small white flies on undersides of leaves	Permethrin
Gnaw roots and soft stems	Trichlorphon or gamma-HCH around plants

Symptoms	Control
Black/brown spots on rose leaves	Bupirimate plus triforine, propiconazole, benomyl or thiophanate-methyl
A greyish fungus on leaves, flowers, etc.	Benomyl, thiophanate-methyl
Yellow leaves, stunted growth on limy soils	Grow in acid soil, apply Sequestrene to soil
Brown spots on leaves	Bupirimate plus triforine, or benomyl
White powdery patches on leaves and shoots	As above, or propiconazole or thiophanate-methyl
Orange or brown spots on undersides of leaves	Bupirimate plus triforine, or propiconazole
Yellow mottling or streaking on leaves, stunted or distorted growth	No cure—destroy affected plants

SPECIAL PROBLEMS

It is not only pests and diseases that can harm your plants. The elements, too, take their toll. If you know what types of problems wind, sun and atmospheric pollution can create for your plants, you can take effective preventative action.

WIND

This can be a problem on roofs and in the gaps between houses (these can become wind tunnels). Dry winds can cause 'scorching' of leaves, wilting, and rapid drying of soil and compost. Wind barriers, however, can be erected to protect vulnerable plants (see pages 14-15).

Semi-permeable barriers or screens—trelliswork and pierced screen-block walling—will filter the wind and slow it down. These can be used to screen a patio partially and should be erected on the windward side.

SUN

Full sun can rapidly dry out compost and soil and may be a problem on roof gardens and patios, since these are generally sited in the sunniest possible spot. Dry soil causes wilting of plants, so growth is checked; leaves and buds may also drop. Some plants are particularly intolerant of drying out—camellias, for instance, which will drop their flower buds.

The solution here is to pay regular attention to watering, particularly with hanging baskets and other containers. It is best to check twice a day in hot weather —morning and evening.

In such a situation, it is, of course, sensible to choose plants that like full sun, avoiding shade-loving plants, which will make only very poor growth. Most summer bedding plants like full sun, as do most bulbs, alpines, silver-leaved herbaceous plants, many shrubs, most of the climbing plants, and roses.

Above: *One of the problems with roof gardens, such as this one in a large city, is that plants are prone to wind, sun and pollution. These problems, however, can be overcome.*

HOLIDAY CARE

There is no way that you can leave plants in containers for a week or two in the summer to fend for themselves. Ideally ask neighbours to check daily (and do the same for them, too).

You could, alternatively, set up an automatic watering system: a trickle or drip irrigation system supplied by a reservoir bottle or bag will keep containers moist for a few days, depending on the size of the reservoir. A system which runs off the mains water supply will allow you to go away for a much longer period without troubling neighbours.

If you have a lot of small pots, stand them on a piece of capillary matting. One end of the matting should be placed in a

bowl of water placed slightly higher than the plants. If the plants are kept in a shady spot they will keep moist for days.

CITY POLLUTION

In cities, towns and industrialized areas, plants may be affected by smoke, factory fumes and traffic fumes. The leaves can become covered in grime, which not only spoils their appearance but adversely affects growth.

Such pollution also affects rain: contaminated rain is popularly known as acid rain and can fall in built-up or country areas. It pollutes the soil, making it less suitable for plant growth, and affected plants lack vigour. It also affects plants in other ways—it can, for example, cause leaf drop, brown or yellow spotting on leaves, and brown leaf edges.

If you live in this type of area, you must choose plants that tolerate pollution and acid rain. Deciduous subjects are a better choice than evergreens, together with herbaceous plants, bulbs, grasses, many alpines,and spring and summer bedding plants.

The following shrubs tolerate polluted rain: hydrangeas, laurels, ivies, euonymus, mahonias, buddleias, hamamelis, Virginia creeper (parthenocissus), berberis, *Erica carnea* varieties, fatsia, forsythia, hollies, roses, hebes and pyracantha. The ornamental and fruiting trees, malus and prunus, are also tolerant.

In polluted areas, spray plants regularly with water to keep them free from grime.

ROOT PROTECTION

Some plants do not like their roots frozen solid, including camellias and any plants that are on the tender side, such as agapanthus. If grown in containers, surround these with dry straw or bracken for the winter to help prevent the compost from freezing solid. Small pots can be plunged to their rims in soil to prevent freezing.

HERBACEOUS PERENNIALS

Few people think of growing herbaceous perennials in containers. It is not clear why, for many are ideally suited to this form of cultivation. Most die down in winter, and are at their best in spring or summer.

WHY GROW PERENNIALS?

Perennial plants make an excellent contrast to the woody plants, such as shrubs, trees and climbers, because they have a completely different habit of growth.

In the main, perennials to be recommended are those with 'architectural' qualities—plants with some definite shape, such as bold foliage, grassy or sword-like foliage, or stately flower spikes. There is no reason why many of the small carpeting and creeping perennials should not be used too, perhaps for training over the edge of containers. Alpines of all kinds are well-suited to container growing.

Also to be recommended are perennials that prefer very well-drained or drier conditions, rather than the moisture-loving kinds. It is difficult to keep the latter completely happy in containers, unless they are planted in large raised beds, which can be kept really moist.

SPECIAL NEEDS

With good drainage in mind, try growing herbaceous perennials in an open, well-aerated, soil-based compost, such as John Innes potting compost No. 2. Do not be too generous with feeding perennials in containers, for this can lead to very soft, tall growth, uncharacteristic of the plants. Feeding about once a month will be sufficient.

GENERAL CARE

Although they like well-drained conditions, do not allow the compost to dry out—keep it moist in spring and summer.

HERBACEOUS PERENNIALS	
Name	**Sun/shade**
Acanthus spinosus	Both
Agapanthus 'Headbourne Hybrids'	Sun
Alchemilla mollis	Sun/partial shade
Bergenia cordifolia	Sun/partial shade
Campanula persicifolia	Sun/partial shade
Chrysanthemum (pompoms)	Sun
Dahlias (dwarf bedding)	Sun
Delphinium hybrids	Sun
Euphorbia wulfenii	Sun/partial shade
Grasses	Sun/partial shade
Helleborus orientalis	Both
Hemerocallis hybrids	Sun/partial shade
Hostas (many varieties)	Shade, partial shade
Kniphofia 'Royal Standard'	Full sun
Lupin 'Russell Hybrids'	Full sun
Phormiums	Sun/partial shade
Rogersia pinnata 'Superba'	Sun/partial shade

The stems of most (unless they are evergreen perennials, such as bergenia) will die down in the autumn, at which stage they should be cut down to almost compost level—just above the dormant growth buds. During the

Left: *Groups of herbaceous perennials look good planted around a patio, like these blue salvias, yellow achilleas, silver cinerarias and pink malva. All of these need a warm sunny position.*

growing season remove dead leaves, and cut off dead flowers —more may then follow. Any plants that produce tall flower spikes may need supporting with bamboo canes; provide one cane per spike for plants such as delphiniums. Most of those listed, though, are self-supporting.

Use slug pellets liberally in the spring, for slugs and snails are very partial to the soft young growth, especially the shoots of hostas and delphiniums.

Foliage	Flowers/season	Height/spread
Deep green, divided	Mauve/white Summer	36 x 24in (90 x 60cm)
Strap-like	Blue shades Summer/autumn	3 x 3ft (1 x 1m)
Rounded, downy	Green-yellow Summer	18 x 18in (45 x 45cm)
Large, rounded, evergreen	Deep pink Spring	12 x 24in (30 x 60cm)
	Blue Summer	36 x 18in (90 x 45cm)
	Many colours Autumn	24 x 24in (60 x 60cm)
	Many colours Summer/autumn	24 x 24in (60 x 60cm)
	Blue, white, purple Summer	Up to 6ft x 18in (2m x 45cm)
Greyish	Green-yellow Spring/summer	48 x 24in (120 x 60cm)
Green, grey, variegated white/gold	Spring/summer	Dwarf to tall
Fingered, evergreen	Pink, purple, white	18 x 24in (45 x 60cm)
Rush-like	Many colours Summer/autumn	30 x 24in (75 x 60cm)
Large, shades of green, greyish, variegated white or gold	White, mauve, lilac Spring-autumn	24 x 24in (60 x 60cm)
Grassy	Yellow, scarlet Summer	3 x 2ft (90 x 60cm)
Fingered	Many colours Summer	30 x 18in (76 x 45cm)
Sword-like, evergreen, plain green, bronze or striped various colours		1-6ft x 1-6ft (30cm-2m x 30cm-2m)
Large, hand-like, bronze	Pink Spring/summer	18 x 18in (45 x 45cm)

SHRUBS AND CLIMBERS

In any planting scheme you need a few larger plants and these could well be shrubs and climbers. Climbers, of course are especially useful for clothing walls, fences, pergolas and other structures. A few largish specimen shrubs provide a framework and additional height to a group of plants.

SPECIAL NEEDS

Shrubs and climbers, being long-term plants, need a substantial compost and, wherever possible, this should be a soil-based kind, such as John Innes potting compost No. 2 or 3.

Bear in mind that some shrubs, including acers, camellias and rhododendrons, need an acid or lime-free compost. If you grow hydrangeas and want blue flowers, then again plant in acid compost.

One of the plants in the list is tender—the oleander (*Nerium oleander*), a popular plant in Mediterranean countries. In colder climates it must be kept in a frost-free greenhouse over winter, but it will be happy out of doors in the summer months. The palm *Trachycarpus fortunei* is normally hardy, but it needs to be sheltered from cold winds.

Camellias should not be in a position where they receive early morning sun, and acers and *Laurus nobilis* (the sweet bay) need shelter from cold winds.

GENERAL CARE

As most of these plants will end up in large containers, they should be topdressed with fresh compost in the spring each year. Every few years they will benefit from repotting into fresh compost, once they are in final containers.

Remove the dead flowers of camellias, daphne, hibiscus, hydrangea, oleander and rhododendrons.

Regular feeding throughout the growing season will be appreciated by all these plants.

Name	Sun/shade
Acer palmatum 'Atropurpureum'	Partial shade
Camellia japonica	Partial shade
Chamaecyparis lawsoniana 'Ellwoodii'	Sun/partial shade
Clematis hybrids and species	Sun (roots in shade)
Daphne odora 'Aureomarginata'	Sun
Elaeagnus pungens 'Maculata'	Sun/partial shade
Euonymus fortunei varieties	Sun/partial shade
Fatsia japonica	Sun/partial shade
Hedera varieties (ivies)	Both
Hibiscus syriacus	Full sun
Hydrangea macrophylla	Partial shade
Jasminum nudiflorum (Winter jasmine)	Sun/partial shade
Juniperus 'Skyrocket'	Sun/partial shade
Juniperus sabina 'Tamariscifolia'	Sun/partial shade
Laurus nobilis (Sweet bay)	Sun
Lonicera periclymenum 'Belgica' (honeysuckle)	Sun, roots in shade
Nerium oleander	Full sun
Parthenocissus (Virginia creeper)	Sun or shade
Prunus laurocerasus 'Otto Luyken'	Both
Rhododendrons and evergreen azaleas	Sun/partial shade
Taxus baccata 'Fastigiata'	Both
Trachycarpus fortunei (hardy palm)	Full sun
Viburnum davidii	Shade/partial shade
Vitis vinifera 'Brant' (grape vine)	Full sun
Yuccas	Full sun

Foliage	Flowers/season	Height/spread
Lobed, purple	Summer/autumn	6 x 6ft (2 x 2m)
Evergreen, deep green, glossy	Pink, red, white Winter/spring	8 x 8ft (2·4 x 2·4m)
Grey-green, feathery, evergreen	All year	6 x 3ft (2 x 1m)
	Many colours Spring-autumn	Climbers, very variable
Evergreen, variegated yellow	Red-purple, fragrant Spring	4 x 5ft (1·2 x 1·5m)
Evergreen, variegated gold	All year	5 x 6ft (1·5 x 1·8m)
Evergreen, often variegated	All year	18 x 24in (45 x 60cm)
Large, hand-like, glossy, evergreen	All year	6 x 6ft (2 x 2m)
Evergreen, lobed, often variegated	All year	Climbers and trailers, very variable
	Many colours Summer/autumn	6 x 6ft (2 x 2m)
	Blue, red, pink, white Summer/autumn	5 x 6ft (1·5 x 2m)
	Yellow Winter	14 x 14ft (4 x 4m) climber
Evergreen, blue-grey	All year	6 x 1ft (180 x 30cm)
Evergreen, bright green, feathery	All year	1 x 4ft (30 x 120cm)
Evergreen, oval, deep green, aromatic	All year	5 x 8ft (1·5 x 2·4m)
	Yellow and red-purple scented. Spring/summer	15 x 10ft (4·5 x 3m) climber
Evergreen, leathery, lance-shaped	Pink, red, cream, white Summer/autumn	6 x 10ft (2 x 3m)
Lobed, scarlet in autumn	Best in autumn	24 x 20ft (7 x 6m)
Evergreen, narrow deep green, glossy	White Spring	4 x 6ft (1·2 x 1·8m)
Evergreen	Many colours Spring	From 12in to 8ft (30cm to 2·4m)
Evergreen, deep green	All year	8 x 2ft (2·4m x 60cm)
Large fan-shaped leaves, evergreen	All year	6-10ft x 6ft (2-3m x 2m)
Oval, deep green, evergreen	Summer/autumn	30in x 4ft (75 x 120cm)
Autumn tints	Edible black grapes in autumn	30ft (9m) plus (climber)
Sword-shaped, evergreen, some variegated	White/cream Year-round interest	3-6ft x 3-6ft (1-2m x 1-2m)

SPRING AND SUMMER BEDDING PLANTS

Hardy and half-hardy annuals, perennials and biennials are indispensable for providing colour in containers of all kinds.

HARDY ANNUALS

These are sown in the open in spring in the position where they are to flower. After flowering, they set seeds and die. They are ideal for quick summer colour —and cheap, too. Try them in containers and planting areas around patios, and dwarf ones can even be inserted into spaces in the paving itself.

HALF-HARDY ANNUALS

Short-lived half-hardy annuals will not tolerate frost, so they are raised from seeds in a heated greenhouse and then planted outside in late spring. They provide lashings of colour in containers on the patio or anywhere in the garden.

HARDY BIENNIALS

Popularly known as spring bedding plants, these are raised from seeds sown one year (in early summer, outdoors), and planted in autumn of the same year. They then flower in the following spring and die.

Some subjects are, strictly, perennial in habit (they live for a number of years) but even these are generally discarded after flowering.

HALF-HARDY PERENNIALS

These plants live for a number of years in their countries of origin, but they will not tolerate frosts. They can be planted out for the summer, and wintered in a frost-free greenhouse. Some kinds, such as pelargoniums and fuchsias, are usually discarded after flowering, new plants being raised from seeds or cuttings each year. Some types can be raised from seed

HARDY ANNUALS (summer)	
Name	Sun/shade
Alyssum maritimum	Sun
Calendula officinalis	Sun
Dimorphotheca aurantiaca	Sun
Iberis umbellata	Sun
Ionopsidium acaule	Partial shade
Leptosiphon hybridus	Sun
Limnanthus douglasii	Sun
Linaria maroccana	Sun
Nemophila insignis	Sun/partial shade
Phacelia campanularia	Sun
Tropaeolum (nasturtium)	Sun

HALF-HARDY ANNUALS (summer)	
Name	Sun/shade
Ageratum houstonianum	Sun
Gazania x hybrida	Sun
Impatiens walleriana	Light or partial shade
Lobelia erinus	Sun/light shade
Mesembryanthemum criniflorum	Sun
Mimulus hybrids	Light or partial shade
Nemesia strumosa	Sun
Nicotiana alata	Sun
Petunia x hybrida	Sun
Salvia splendens	Sun
Tagetes erecta	Sun
Tagetes patula	Sun
Verbena x hybrida	Sun

Foliage	Flowers	Height/spread
	White, pink, purple, red, sweetly scented	4 x 8in (10 x 20cm)
Aromatic leaf	Orange, yellow shades	12-18in x 12-18in (30-45cm x 30-45cm)
	Many colours	12-18in x 12in (30-45cm x 30cm)
	Range of bright colours	6-12in x 8in (15-30cm x 20cm)
	Pale mauve	2 x 6in (5 x 15cm)
Deeply divided	Many colours	4-6in x 4in (10-15cm x 10cm)
Bright green	Yellow and white	4 x 6in (10 x 15cm)
	Many bright colours	8-18in x 6in (20-45cm x 15cm)
Feathery leaves	Blue and white	8 x 6in (20 x 15cm)
	Blue	8 x 6in (20 x 15cm)
Large rounded	Many bright colours	6-12in (15-30cm) high, trailing habit

Foliage	Flowers	Height/spread
	Blue, white, purplish	4-12in x 6-8in (10-30cm x 15-20cm)
Deep green and grey	Orange and yellow shades	8-12in x 12in (20-30cm x 30cm)
	Many colours	6-12in x 8-12in (15-30cm x 20-30cm)
	Blue, red, white	4-8in (10-20cm) high compact or trailing
Fleshy leaves	Many colours	4 x 6in (10 x 15cm)
	Red, yellow and orange shades	6-12in x 6-8in (15-30cm x 15-20cm)
	Many colours	8-18in x 6-8in (20-45cm x 15-20cm)
Sticky leaves	Fragrant, many colours	10-36in x 8-12in (25-90cm x 20-30cm)
	Many colours	6-12in x 12in (15-30cm x 30cm)
	Scarlet, pink, purple	12in x 6-8in (30cm x 15-20cm)
Aromatic leaves	Many yellow and orange shades	12-36in x 8-12in (30-90cm x 20-30cm)
Aromatic leaves	Many yellow, orange and red shades	6-12in x 6-12in (15-30cm x 15-30cm)
	Many colours	6-12in x 12in (15-30cm x 30cm)

SPRING AND SUMMER BEDDING PLANTS

in a heated greenhouse, while others are usually bought in.

CARE OF BEDDING PLANTS

Most of these plants need well-drained compost and plenty of sun. The soil/compost should not be very rich or it will result in lush foliage but few flowers.

Dead-heading on a regular basis is highly recommended, since this results in continuous flowering. If biennials are lifted by frosts, re-firm them as soon as the soil has thawed out.

HARDY BIENNIALS (spring flowering)
Name
Bellis perennis 'Monstrosa'
Cheiranthus cheiri
Cheiranthus allionii
Myosotis alpestris
Polyanthus
Viola x *wittrockiana*

HALF-HARDY PERENNIALS (summer flowering)		
Name	**Foliage**	**Flowers**
Abutilon striatum 'Thompsonii'	Large yellow-mottled leaves	Orange
Agave americana 'Marginata'	Rosette of sword-shaped leaves, edged yellow	
Begonia semperflorens	Some have bronze leaves	Red, pink, white
Canna x *generalis*	Large, green or purple	Orange, red yellow
Chlorophytum elatum 'Variegatum'	Grassy, striped green and white	White
Cineraria maritima	Silvery-grey ferny leaves	
Coleus blumei	Multi-coloured foliage	
Cordyline australis	Long, narrow, grey-green leaves	
Echeveria glauca	Rosette of fleshy greyish leaves	Red
Eucalyptus globulus	Aromatic grey leaves	
Fuchsias		Many colours
Heliotropium x *hybridum*		Shades of violet and blue
Iresine species	Red or yellow leaves	
Pelargoniums (zonal)	Often zoned bronze or multicoloured	Red, pink orange, white
Pelargoniums (ivy-leaf)	Ivy-shaped leaves	Red, pink or white
Ricinus communis	Large palmate leaves, green or bronze	Green

Sun/shade	Flowers	Height/spread
Sun or partial shade	Pink, red, white	6 x 6in (15 x 15cm)
Sun	Fragrant, many colours	8-24in x 12in (20-60cm x 30cm)
Sun	Shades of orange and yellow	12 x 12in (30 x 30cm)
Partial shade or sun	Shade of blue, pink or white	6-8in x 6in (15-20cm x 15cm)
Shade, partial shade or sun	Many colours	6-8in x 6-8in (15-20cm x 15-20cm)
Sun or partial shade	Many colours	6 x 6in (15 x 15cm)

Long-term plant	Generally seed-raised	Sun/ shade	Height/spread
Yes	No	Sun	4ft x 3-4ft (1·2m x 1-1·2m)
Yes	No	Sun	3 x 3ft (1 x 1m)
No	Yes	Sun or light shade	8-12in x 8in (20-30cm x 20cm)
Yes	No	Sun	2-4ft x 2-3ft (60-120cm x 60-90cm)
Yes	No	Sun or light shade	12 x 18in (30 x 45cm)
No	Yes	Sun or light shade	12 x 12in (30 x 30cm)
No	Yes	Sun	12 x 12in (30 x 30cm)
Yes	No	Sun or light shade	2-3ft x 2-3ft (60-90cm x 60-90cm)
Yes	No	Sun	3 x 4in (7·5 x 10cm)
Yes	Yes	Sun	3-6ft x 18-24in (1-2m x 45-60cm)
If desired	No	Sun or light shade	Average 18 x 18in (45 x 45cm)
No	Yes	Sun	12-18in x 12-18in (30-45cm x 30-45cm)
No	No	Sun	12 x 12in (30 x 30cm)
If desired	If desired	Sun	12-18in x 12-18in (30-45cm x 30-45cm)
If desired	No	Sun	12 x 18in (30 x 45cm)
No	Yes	Sun	5 x 3ft (150 x 90cm)

ROSES

Roses are popular, long-lived, easy, reliable, give plenty of colour and often fragrance. Moreover, they are versatile, growing just as well in containers as in beds. Climbing roses can be used to clothe walls, fences and trellis.

SPECIAL NEEDS

For containers, choose short compact bush roses and the smaller, less vigorous climbers. Good soil drainage is absolutely essential, as is rich soil; so fill containers with John Innes potting compost No. 3. Choose pots or tubs at least 12in (30cm) deep and with a similar diameter. Ideally use clay pots or wooden tubs, rather than plastic, and position each container in full sun.

GENERAL CARE

It is best not to put roses direct into 12in (30cm) containers, but pot them on when they are dormant. Annually, in spring, scrape off a little compost when the plants are in their final containers and replace with fresh compost. Roses need to be kept steadily moist in spring and summer, and benefit from monthly feeding in the growing season with a rose fertilizer.

Rigorously control pests and

Above: *All of the miniature roses are suitable for growing in containers or raised beds.*
Right: *Climbing roses like 'Golden Showers' are invaluable for clothing walls and fences. Choose the smaller, less-vigorous kinds for containers and raised beds.*

diseases (see pages 52-53) and carry out regular pruning (see pages 48-49). With such care and attention roses will remain vigorous and free-flowering for many years.

Type	Flower Colour/Recommended Varieties
Large flowered bush roses (hybrid teas)	Very wide range of colours 'Isobel Harkness' (yellow), 'Just Joey' (copper), 'National Trust' (red)
Cluster-flowered bush roses (floribundas)	Very wide range of colours 'Anna Ford' (orange), 'Peek a Boo' (apricot)
Climbers	Very wide range of colours 'Aloha' (pink), 'Copenhagen' (dark scarlet) 'Golden Showers' (yellow)
Ramblers	A very good choice of colours 'Crimson Showers' (red), 'Leverkusen' (yellow) —ideal for a north or east facing wall
Miniature roses	Many colours are now available 'Baby Gold Star' (yellow), 'Colibri' (apricot) 'Pour Toi' (cream), 'Robin' (red)

Fragrance	Height and Spread
Many are, but by no means all	Choose lower-growing kinds; approx. 30 x 30in (75 x 75cm)
A comparatively small number are scented	Choose lower-growing kinds; approx. 18 x 18in (45 x 45cm)
Many are strongly scented	Choose the less-vigorous, smaller-growing kinds; approx. 6 x 6ft (1·8 x 1·8m)
Some are scented, but choose carefully	Choose the smaller less-vigorous kinds, as some are excessively vigorous; approx. 6 x 6ft (1·8 x 1·8m)
A few are scented but this is not their main attraction	All miniature roses are suitable for containers; approx 12 x 12in (30 x 30cm)

VEGETABLES AND HERBS

A patio, balcony or roof garden need not be only decorative—it can also be productive. Many vegetables and herbs are suited to growing in containers, which can be tucked away in any convenient free space.

Most of the plants listed are ideal for growing bags. These should be used once only, or twice at most—for instance, a crop of winter lettuces could follow a summer crop of tomatoes.

Large pots—say, 12in (30cm) in diameter—may also be used, and can be particularly recommended for crops such as aubergines, capsicums, cucumbers, okra, tomatoes, and the

VEGETABLES	
Name	**Sowing/planting time**
Aubergine	Sow early spring, plant late spring
Bean—dwarf French	Sow late spring
Beetroot	Sow early spring to mid summer
Capsicum (sweet pepper)	Sow early spring, plant late spring
Carrots	Sow early spring to early summer
Celtuce	Sow mid-late spring
Corn salad	Sow late summer
Cucumber	Sow mid spring, plant late spring
Endive	Sow mid spring to early autumn
Lettuce	Sow early spring to mid autumn
Okra	Sow early spring, plant mid-late spring
Onion (spring or salad)	Sow early-late spring
Peas	Sow late winter or early spring
Radishes	Sow early spring to early autumn
Tomato	Sow early spring, plant mid-late spring

HERBS	
Name	**Sowing/planting time**
Chives	Sow or plant in spring
Mint	Plant roots in spring
Parsley	Sow early spring to mid summer
Rosemary	Plant in spring
Sage	Sow or plant in spring
Thyme	Sow or plant in spring

herbs. All the herbs listed, except parsley, are perennial. Parsley can, if desired, be grown in special parsley pots with planting holes in the sides. These pots can be very attractive and will make a decorative addition to a sunny window sill.

Fill pots with John Innes potting compost No. 2 or 3. Mint likes moist conditions and would do well in a peat-based potting compost.

Tall plants in growing-bags, such as tomatoes, aubergines, capsicums and cucumbers, can be supported with proprietary growing-bag crop supports. Feed and water all crops well during the summer growing season.

Plant spacing	Comments
18 x 18in (45 x 45cm)	Best results when grown under glass
12 x 12in (30 x 30cm)	Pick beans regularly once cropping starts
4 x 4in (10 x 10cm)	Use round-rooted varieties for containers
18 x 18in (45 x 45cm)	Best results when grown under glass
2 x 2in (5 x 5cm)	Grow only round or stump-rooted varieties in containers
6 x 6in (15 x 15cm)	A substitute for lettuce and quick growing
4 x 4in (10 x 10cm)	Leaves used like lettuce—useful for autumn and winter
24 x 24in (60 x 60cm)	Choose the ridge or outdoor varieties
12 x 12in (30 x 30cm)	Varieties for summer and autumn use—a substitute for lettuce
12 x 12in (30 x 30cm)	Sow summer and winter lettuce for a long supply
18 x 18in (45 x 45cm)	Needs glass protection or warm sheltered spot
No thinning needed	Pull as soon as large enough to use
3 x 3in (7·5 x 7·5cm)	Choose dwarf early maturing varieties
1 x 1in (2·5 x 2·5cm)	Sow in succession for a long supply
18 x 18in (45 x 45cm)	Grow outdoor varieties, including the dwarf bush kinds

Plant spacing	Comments
Clumps about 6 x 6in (15 x 15cm)	Use the leaves for onion flavourings
6 x 6in (15 x 15cm)	Leaves often used for making mint sauce
6 x 6in (15 x 15cm)	Leaves used for garnishing and flavouring
Single plant sufficient	Leaves used in meat casseroles, particularly lamb
12 x 12in (30 x 30cm)	Leaves used for flavouring meats
8 x 8in (20 x 20cm)	Leaves used to flavour meats, poultry and game

FRUIT

With the introduction of new dwarf varieties, growing fruits in containers is becoming increasingly popular and it is well worthwhile, since they give good returns from the space they occupy. Freshly picked fruits are undeniably superior to shop-bought produce and, as an added bonus, most plants also make decorative features on a patio, terrace or roof garden.

SUITABLE TREES

Modern dwarfing rootstocks allow small trees to be grown, and even cherries have now been suitably dwarfed for container work. Most fruits are grown as dwarf bush trees or dwarf pyramids and do not take up a great deal of lateral space. Some nursery-men supply apples and pears as 'family trees', with several varieties on one tree—ideal for those with very limited space.

Right: *Peaches, grown as bush trees, are ideally suited to cultivation in containers.*

SPECIAL NEEDS

All need a warm, sunny, sheltered position. Citrus fruits are tender so need to be overwintered in a frost-free greenhouse or room. Figs also need winter protection to avoid the embryo fruits being killed by frost.

Fruit	Varieties
Apples	'Ashmead's Kernel', 'Cox's Orange Pippin', 'Disc 'Egremont Russet', 'Greensleeves'
Blackcurrants	'Ben Lomond', 'Ben Nevis'
Cherries	'Stella'
Citrus fruits	*Citrus aurantium* (Seville orange) and *C. sinensis* (sweet orange)
Figs	'Brown Turkey', 'White Marseilles'
Gooseberries	'Leveller', 'Whinham's Industry'
Grapes	'Black Hamburg'
Nectarines	'Lord Napier'
Peaches	'Hale's Early', 'Duke of York'
Pears	'Doyenne du Comice' grown with 'Beurré Hardy'; 'Conference' grown with 'Williams' Bon Chrétien'
Plums	'Victoria'
Raspberries	'Malling Jewel', 'Glen Clova'
Strawberries	'Aromel', 'Vigour'

To ensure cross-pollination of the flowers of apples or pears (and hence good crops of fruit) grow several varieties of the same fruit together. Hand pollinate the flowers of peaches and nectarines, using a soft artist's brush.

Use clay pots, 12-15in (30-38cm) in diameter, to start with and gradually move the plants into larger containers. Fill with John Innes potting compost No. 3 and place plenty of drainage material in the bottom. Grow strawberries in strawberry barrels or tower-pots.

GENERAL CARE

Avoid allowing the compost to dry out or to become very wet, and liquid feed weekly in the growing season with a high-potash fertilizer. Early flowers can be protected from frost by draping the trees with windbreak netting at night. Thin out the fruits so that the trees do not carry excessively heavy crops, for this will reduce crops in subsequent years.

For pruning, refer to a specialist fruit book. Pot on as required in late autumn—the final container size should be 18-24in (45·5-60cm). Trees in final containers should be repotted each year to replace the old compost with fresh material. Plunge or insulate pots to protect the soil from freezing in winter.

Form of training	Comments
Dwarf bush or dwarf pyramid	These cross-pollinate each other. Buy trees on dwarfing rootstock M.9 or M.27
Bushes	Cut out fruiting shoots immediately after fruiting
Bush trees or dwarf pyramid	A self-fertile variety. Buy tree on dwarfing rootstock 'Colt'
Bush trees or dwarf pyramid	Keep frost-free over winter
Bush trees	Keep frost-free over winter
Bush on short stem (leg)	Cut new growth back by half in late autumn
Grow as a standard, about 6ft (1·8m) high	The head is cut back each winter
Bush trees	Hand pollinate the flowers
Bush trees	Hand pollinate the flowers
Dwarf bush or dwarf pyramid	These varieties are paired up for effective cross-pollination
Dwarf bush or dwarf pyramid	This variety is self-fertile. Buy tree on dwarf rootstock 'Pixy'
One plant per container, with 5-6 shoots trained on canes or wires	Cut fruiting shoots down to ground level after fruiting
	Grow in strawberry barrel or Tower-Pot

SMALL ORNAMENTAL TREES

Small ornamental trees are well suited to container growing, and they can also be planted in a border or bed in or near a patio. These plants are ideal for providing a variation in height and added interest in and around a sitting area. They can also provide useful shade. There is a choice between weeping trees or fastigate (vertically growing) types.

CHOOSING TREES

Container growing will restrict the size of trees, although some may eventually grow too large for even the biggest pot. It is best to choose the slower-growing species and varieties.

SPECIAL NEEDS

The requirements of ornamental trees are much the same as those of fruit trees (see pages 70-71). They should be grown in clay pots to start with, then moved by degrees into large pots or tubs with a diameter and depth of at least 24in (60cm). Trees can also be grown in raised beds. Use John Innes potting compost No. 3 for containers.

GENERAL CARE

Keep well watered in dry weather to prevent the compost drying out, and feed about once a fortnight with liquid fertilizer in the growing season. Very little pruning is needed—the removal of dead and damaged shoots is all that should be necessary. Otherwise, general care is the same as for fruit trees.

Right: *This variegated holly, a variety of* Ilex aquifolium, *is a good choice for containers as it is slow growing and has a very compact habit of growth.*
Far right: *Small ornamental trees like Robinia 'Frisia' provide variation in height and, of course, shade in hot weather.*

Name	Berries
Cotoneaster 'Hybridus Pendulus'	Red
Crataegus oxyacantha 'Paul's Scarlet'	
Malus floribunda	Yellow
Prunus 'Amanogawa'	
Pyrus salicifolia 'Pendula'	
Robinia pseudoacacia 'Frisia'	
Salix caprea 'Pendula'	
Sorbus 'Joseph Rock'	Yellow

Foliage	Flowers/season	Height/spread
Evergreen, oval, shiny	White Summer-autumn	Grafted on stem 6 x 6ft (1·8 x 1·8m)
Deciduous	Scarlet Spring	15 x 15ft (4·5 x 4·5m)
Ovate, deciduous	Pale pink Spring/autumn	12 x 10ft (3·6 x 3m)
Deciduous	Pale pink Spring	20 x 3ft (6 x 1m)
Willow-like, silvery, deciduous	Cream Spring-summer	15 x 10ft (4·5 x 3m)
Golden, deciduous	Spring-summer	18 x 12ft (5·4 x 3·6m)
Elliptical, deciduous	Yellow catkins Spring-summer	10 x 10ft (3 x 3m)
Ferny, good autumn colour, deciduous	White Spring/autumn	18 x 8ft (5·4 x 2·4m)

BULBS

Bulbs are among the easiest plants to grow, and they are ideally suited to cultivation in containers of all shapes and sizes. All bulbs need good drainage; therefore ensure that containers have plenty of drainage material in their bases. Bulbs can be grown in both soil-based and soilless composts.

Plant spring-flowering bulbs (plus lilies) in late summer and autumn, and most summer- and autumn-flowering bulbs in spring.

When flowering is over, bulbs will benefit from several liquid feeds, using a compound fertilizer, to help build them up for next year. Leave the foliage intact until it has completely died down.

SPRING BULBS

Name	Flower colour/season	Sun/shade
Chionodoxa	Blue; early spring	Sun
Crocuses (large flowered)	Yellow, purple, white; all spring	Sun
Galanthus (snowdrops)	White; winter-spring	Sun/shade
Hyacinths	Red, pink, blue, yellow, white; all spring	Full sun
Irises (dwarf)	Blue, purple, yellow; early spring	Full sun
Leucojum vernum	White; early spring	Shade
Muscari	Blue; all spring	Sun
Narcissus	Yellow, gold, white and bicolours; all spring	Sun/partial shade
Scilla	Blue; early spring	Sun
Tulips (tall and dwarf)	Many colours; all spring	Full sun

SUMMER AND AUTUMN BULBS

Name	Flower colour/season	Sun/shade
Anemone coronaria	Many colours; late summer	Full sun
Begonia (tuberous)	Many colours; early summer to early autumn	Sun/partial shade
Iris, Dutch	Blue, mauve, yellow, white; early summer	Sun
Lilies	Many colours, some fragrant; all summer	Sun/partial shade
Nerine bowdenii	Pink; early autumn	Full sun
Ranunculus	Many colours; early summer	Sun
Tigridia	Orange-red; late summer	Full sun

If you want to use the containers for other plants, bulbs can be lifted when flowering is over, but don't disturb galanthus, leucojum or nerine. Plant the lifted bulbs shallowly in a spare piece of ground, and keep them watered and fed until the foliage has died down. Then they can be dug up again, cleaned, dried and stored until planting time again.

Two tender subjects are listed here: begonias and tigridias. These should be lifted in autumn before the hard frosts commence, dried off and stored in a frost-proof place over winter. The begonias should be started off in heat and planted out when all danger of frost is over.

Height	Planting distance	Planting depth
3-4in (7·5-10cm)	1in (2·5cm)	3in (7·5cm)
4in (10cm)	3in (7·5cm)	3in (7·5cm)
6-12in (15-30cm)	3in (7·5cm)	3in (7·5cm)
9-12in (23-30cm)	8in (20cm)	4in (10cm)
4-6in (10-15cm)	3in (7·5cm)	4in (10cm)
6in (15cm)	4in (10cm)	3in (7·5cm)
6-8in (15-20cm)	4in (10cm)	3in (7·5cm)
4-24in (10-60cm)	Dwarf: 3in (7·5cm) Tall: 6in (15cm)	Dwarf: 3in (7·5cm) Tall: 6in (15cm)
4in (10cm)	4in (10cm)	3in (7·5cm)
6-24in (15-60cm)	6in (15cm)	4in (10cm)

Height	Planting distance	Planting depth
6-12in (15-30cm)	6in (15cm)	3in (7·5cm)
12in (30cm)	6-8in (15-20cm)	Plant from pots or boxes
24in (60cm)	6in (15cm)	3in (7·5cm)
2-6ft (60cm-2m)	8in (20cm)	6-9in (15-23cm)
18in (45cm)	4in (10cm)	With tips just showing
12in (30cm)	6in (15cm)	3in (7·5cm)
24in (60cm)	6in (15cm)	3in (7.5cm)

INDEX

PICTURE CREDITS

Artists
Copyright of the artwork illustrations on the pages following the artists' names is the property of Salamander Books Ltd.
Janos Marffy: 15, 22, 27, 29, 32, 37, 46, 48, 49, 51, 52, 53
Clifford and Wendy Meadway: 30, 31

Photographs
The publishers wish to thank the following photographers, agencies and companies who have supplied photographs for this book. The photographs have been credited by page number, and position on the page where appropriate: B (Bottom), T (Top), BL (Bottom Left) etc.
Eric Crichton: Endpapers, 4-5, 6, 8, 9, 10, 11, 12, 13, 14, 16, 17, 18, 19, 20, 21, 23, 24, 25, 26, 28(T), 31, 33, 34, 36, 38, 39, 40, 41, 42, 44, 45, 46, 47, 48, 50, 57, 58, 66, 67, 73, Back cover
Brian Furner Horticultural Photographs: 70-71
Tania Midgley: 43, 72
Ken Muir Fruit Ltd: 28(B)

PRINTED IN BELGIUM BY
proost
INTERNATIONAL BOOK PRODUCTION